Hammers Through the Looking Glass
An Alternative History of West Ham United

DESERT ISLAND FOOTBALL HISTORIES

Hammers Through the Looking Glass

AN ALTERNATIVE HISTORY OF WEST HAM UNITED

A NOVEL

Series Editor: Clive Leatherdale

Martin Godleman

DESERT ISLAND BOOKS

First published in 2006
by
DESERT ISLAND BOOKS LIMITED
7 Clarence Road, Southend-on-Sea, Essex SS1 1AN
United Kingdom
www.desertislandbooks.com

© 2006 Martin Godleman

British Library Cataloguing-in-Publication Data
A catalogue record for this book is available from the British Library

ISBN(10) 1-905328-23-0
IBSN(13) 978-905328-23-9

Printed in Great Britain
by
4edge Ltd.

Publisher's Note

The whole world knows Russian linesman Tofik Bakhramov got it wrong in 1966. There are good places to make a mistake and bad places and the World Cup final with millions watching around the globe is not a good place.

With England drawing 2-2 with West Germany in the World Cup final at Wembley, Geoff Hurst pivoted and shot. The ball cannoned down off the crossbar onto the goal-line – photos prove it was not behind it – and back into play, but Bakhramov signalled a goal. A Russian linesman, German victims. Conspiracy theorists have had a field-day ever since.

Let's suppose that Bakhramov got it right, raised his flag and signalled 'no goal'. Who knows how the final might have ended. Had the game, or the replay, eventually gone West Germany's way there would have been several obvious victims. Geoff Hurst would have been denied his unique hat-trick, Alf Ramsey would have been denied his 'I told you so', and his knighthood, and West Ham fans would have been denied the chance to crow that – with three players in the England team – it was the 'ammers what won the World Cup.

This is the starting point for Martin Godleman's *Hammers Through the Looking Glass*. He rewrites history, interweaving fact and fiction to show what might have happened, as opposed to what did.

Hammers Through the Looking Glass is a novel. Most novels disclaim any association with any real persons alive or dead. That is not possible in this case, for most names are real. Nevertheless, what follows is pure invention, and no slight is intended to anyone whose life – without the benefit of Bakhramov's immortal blunder – turns out rather less rosy.

CHAPTER ONE

Decisions, Decisions, Decisions

I am twelve and this day is the most exciting day of my life.

Today, Saturday 30th July 1966. Not only are my country in the World Cup Final against West Germany, but it's the summer holidays – no school for another six weeks.

The other great thing is that I know what's going to happen.
Hardly got any sleep last night, but when I finally dropped off I dreamed this incredible dream. Not only are England going to win today, but Geoff Hurst is going to score a hat-trick. I am so sure of this, that this morning I started to badger my dad about it.

'All three goals.'

'It's a nice thought, son, but not Hurst. Greaves is your man. If Ramsey's got the balls he'll be playing him up with Roger Hunt. He may have been out for a while, but no-one finishes like Greaves. His record speaks for itself.'

'Can't you do something about it, dad? Tell someone about it, a local reporter or something. People will be amazed that you got such a crazy prediction right.'

'They'll be amazed at how crazy I am, I don't doubt it.'

And so it went on. Nobody listens to you when you're a kid. And it doesn't help when everyone in this house supports Spurs. Except me. I don't really support anyone, except England. And I'd love Jimmy Greaves to be there, knocking them in for England, but the dream has said otherwise.

Two hours later comes the news that should have dad ready to shout my predictions up and down the street. The team selection.

'So how did I know Hurst would even be playing?'

'Look, Roy, it isn't going to happen. The way West Germany played against Russia, it'll be difficult for England to get one goal, let alone three.'

'But you've got to admit, dad, he's playing – and he's going to score three goals.'

The game's already started, but my dad won't admit anything. Funny thing is, I know nobody will believe me – until it happens. The whole thing seems so real that I don't need anyone else's reassurance. Not even dad's. It'll be all the more glorious when it happens. Knowing the future gives you a kind of power.

They're all here. My granddad, my Uncle Pete and Barry from next door. Our telly's one of the best in the street. Mum's always moaning about the HP payments, but I think she likes the way it has turned our house into a sort of football shrine these past three weeks.

They're all sitting up at the table, leaning over their beers, while I'm sprawled on the carpet with my mug of tea parked in front of the fireplace. The opinion round the table is that West Germany are too strong for the likes of Ray Wilson and George Cohen. Being as we're watching this from Hendon in North London, the lack of Spurs players in the team is the reason England are bound to lose. Of course no-one is interested in my opinion. Dad has forbidden me to mention the dream about the hat-trick.

And then it happens. Ray Wilson, Mr Reliable as my dad calls him, fails to clear the ball properly with a header that barely makes it to the edge of the area and, twelve minutes in, Helmut Haller, the German striker, rams home the first goal of the game. The West Germans are ahead. This wasn't what I dreamed. But I won't be dispirited. I keep my eyes glued to the screen, my face squashed into folds of skin between my compressed palms. They've already started moaning about a 'bloody Scouser' letting us down, though my dad corrects them as to Ray Wilson being strictly speaking a Midlander who just happens to play for Everton. See, he can be that thorough in his analysis, but he won't accept that I could ...

The ensuing minutes of misery are dispatched into oblivion as a free-kick from Bobby Moore hit towards the far post is met by Hurst's head ... and England are level. More importantly, at least for me, it's goal number one for Geoff Hurst. I daren't look round, because I know my dad is looking at me. Suddenly I feel a little embarrassed for having made what is now looking like a rather elegant prediction. He's only got to score another two, after all. But then Greaves played in all three of the first round matches and didn't even manage one. No goals in 270 minutes, and I'm expecting Hurst to get another two in a quarter of that. Less than that now, as the half-time whistle goes.

'See – he's already got one,' I say to dad, as I go out to the kitchen to get the plate of sandwiches mum has prepared. Dad doesn't answer, but I can see the beginnings of a smile at the corner of his mouth. The joy of still being in the game after conceding such an early goal, I suppose.

The second half is a fraught, nerve-wracking experience. As the minutes tick away, my dream is looking like a nightmare, but finally England take the lead. How could an England goal in a World Cup Final disappoint me? But it does, because although it's Hurst who fires in a shot to the far post, his effort is deflected up into the air for Martin Peters to ram it home on the volley. 2-1 ahead, but how is Hurst going to score another two in the last twelve minutes? The Germans will have to all develop terminal cramp or collapse with a bout of unexpected delayed food poisoning.

I have lost interest in the game, my presence and my dream hidden by the boorish beer-induced singing coming from the dinner table behind me. They don't seem to care that it's three West Ham players who have linked up to score the two goals that are going to win the World Cup for England. They're just delighted to win. And then the Germans are awarded a free-kick just outside the area …

It happens so quickly that I seem to be the only one in the room who's noticed.

'They've scored – dad, the Germans have scored!'

Wolfgang Weber has bundled the ball over the line after a muddle in the England defence, with seconds left on the clock. The room has grown very quiet, and it is in that quiet, gnawing disappointment that I suddenly realise how Hurst is going to find the necessary minutes to score those two goals. Extra time.

I catch dad out in the pantry, opening a few more bottles. Looking out beyond him into the street, I can see a vast concrete wilderness. It's normally only like this on Christmas Day. Everybody, it would seem, is in front of a wireless set or television.

'So what do you reckon, Roy? Pity the powers that be in football haven't sorted out substitutes yet. You know who'd make a difference out there now …'

I make a half smile at my dad. It seems like he's forgotten about our earlier conversation.

Back in the front room the teams are getting ready to go into battle again. This is the time when I start to recognise what a strange giraffe-like body Jack Charlton has, and wonder, looking at Nobby Stiles, just what it must be like to have no teeth. To let your tongue ride up on the roof of your mouth only to reach your lips without any obstacle.

I look down at the hearth and see that dad has made me another cup of tea. Odd that, as I didn't see him pour it.

The game has already restarted and England are on the attack, resuming as they left off. Their dark shirts are still unfamiliar after a tournament of white, and all because of the toss of a coin. Is that what'll happen if it ends up all square by the end of play? There has to be a better way of deciding things. Those endless FA Cup replays with pitches that degenerate into quagmires after staging three games in a week.

Wembley is holding up in the July sunshine. We're watching the game on ITV because dad hates the BBC. 'All run by gentlemen,' he says, which seems to me like it might be a good thing, but it's the issue of 'class' that upsets dad. ITV apparently doesn't make such distinctions. Which is why we're listening to the dulcet tones of Hugh Johns rather than the BBC's Second World War bomber pilot Kenneth Wolstenholme.

The game seems to have slowed down, and it looks as though most of the players didn't plan to be on the pitch for another half an hour. Are we more fit than the Germans? From what they're saying behind me, you'd think it was the Third World War. Maybe Wolstenholme would be better off coming away from his commentary microphone and looking for the nearest bomber plane.

With four minutes to go before the first break, my dream starts to fizz back into life. Alan Ball, the red-headed teenager runs to the byline to pull the ball back into the path of Geoff Hurst, who is onto the pass with perfect timing, slamming it over the West German keeper Tilkowski, but against the underside of the crossbar. The ball bounces out from inside the goal, it seems, and number 21, that's Hunt I'm thinking, runs away from the goal in celebration. The camera homes in on Hurst, whose arm is aloft, it has to be said, without the greatest aura of certainty.

'Goal!' shouts Uncle Pete.

'Yeah!' shouts Barry.

My dad just stares, wearing half the smile I showed him quarter of an hour previously.

'This is it, dad!' I yell. Dad looks at me in horror, though whether it's what I've said or the fact that the referee is marching over to the linesman, it's impossible to say.

'It must be a goal,' says Hugh Johns.

It doesn't exactly sound like the kind of thing a gentleman would say. I imagine Kenneth Wolstenholme's a picture of the level-headed fence sitter on the BBC.

'Can't they show it again?' Barry says.

'Like a replay,' Uncle Pete says, helpfully.

'Look at that bloody linesman,' Barry says. He looks like Joseph Stalin ...'

As he's speaking, I notice on the *Daily Mirror* sports page in front of me that the linesman is Russian. The Russians and the Germans in the war?

Before I can work out a narrative for the likely course of events, the referee is shaking his head and runs away from the corner of the pitch making an umpire's 'dead ball' gesture. Hurst is standing with hands on hips, looking towards the centre of the pitch in disgust. The crowd are delivering a kind of low moaning roar of disdain as the German keeper places the ball for the goal kick that has been awarded.

Although my dream is now almost nine hours old, its discrete components begin to pop up in my head. In my dream, this is Hurst's goal, this is the two-thirds step towards the hat-trick that he will complete in twenty minutes with a left footed pile-driver of a shot on the run to win England the World Cup.

That refereeing decision has draped another veil of silence over the front room. I glance swiftly over my left shoulder to see the glazed stupor of the three men's expressions as they take in what's just been presented on the small screen in front of them.

I didn't even manage to make anything of the moment as it hung there while the men in black stood in solemn conference at the side of the pitch. Has the chance of winning, like my dream, gone forever? Bobby Moore has fouled Overath as he attempts to pass him on the left. The Germans have another free-kick. Banks fields Held's weak shot comfortably, and the whistle goes for the change round.

I jump as my left elbow is grabbed from the side by my mum, pushing

11

a sausage roll on a plate in front of me. I smile weakly, less of a smile even than the one my dad got earlier.

'Come on love, have something to eat. It's nearly tea time.'

Mum has been upstairs, knitting. How can she fail to be even slightly interested in what's going on at Wembley today? But I look round and notice that she's sitting on the settee, my dad making a determined effort to explain what has been happening to her.

'What if no-one scores again?' she says finally, at the end of his sermon.

The men all look at each other. No-one seems to know. It'll be a replay. Won't it?

'He had a long hard look,' Hugh Johns is saying, 'but when there's a benefit of the doubt to be given, it's the defending team who are more likely to get it …'

The two teams have just kicked off for the second period of extra time, and I'm reflecting on what my mum has just said. The last fifteen minutes are played out with England trying everything possible to find a way through the German defence, but apart from a Bobby Charlton shot from twenty-five yards that narrowly clears the bar, there is no clear chance for either side.

The camera follows the players off the field, but Hugh Johns and whoever is sitting in the commentary box with him spend a further ten minutes of the broadcast speculating about Hurst's effort at the end of the first period of extra time. The tape editors manage to show the incident again, several times, but it's no more conclusive than it was when I saw it live. Both teams manage a lap of honour, but there's nothing else to report.

'Still,' dad says, finally, as he switches the television off. 'At least we didn't have to win it on a controversial decision like that. You'd have never heard the last of it from the Germans if we had.'

Uncle Pete and Barry are on their way within quarter of an hour, and the house returns to the kind of fidgety silence that it bathes in on most Sunday evenings during the winter.

It's hard for me to let the whole thing go. The dream sits in my memory as a serious rival to the truth that we have just witnessed, lying there as if it might make a fight of it. For all we know, Hurst may well have gone on to score another if his effort had been judged as having crossed the line. And what of Alf Ramsey, the man who declared with a scarcely credible confidence that England would win the World Cup? How is he going to motivate his players after something like that?

Well at least I know now that the match is going to be replayed on Tuesday – just over a fortnight before the new football season begins.

I have started playing football outside the back of our house. Kicking a ball against the back wall, lobbing it into the three chalk circles I've marked, one after the other, until I get to the magic ninety-nine, and then I volley it up as hard as I can, as far as I can, aiming to clear the four rows of garden fences behind the house. Then the search to get to where it's landed and retrieve it before the kids from the other side of the estate get their hands on it.

Unfortunately, this game has yet to reach its climax. I think I've made it too difficult, as I've yet to hit the circle more than seven times in succession. The disappointment spurs me on, though, which is beyond logic, because I don't seem to be getting any better. There aren't many things in life like football for seizing your imagination and refusing to let go, choking it almost as you wonder where the rest of your life went.

The football writers are at it first thing Monday.

'Hurst Heartbreak!'

'Ramsey's Renegades Fall At Last Hurdle'

'Russian Linesman Betrays England'

That last one made my dad laugh, for some reason. He says that the Russians have short memories. I can't really see what football has got to do with the War. We're only facing half of the Germans, after all. And from what I can see, the Russians have half of Germany under their noses already – what would they want with the other half?

I should be looking in a forward direction to this match, but I keep finding myself looking back at Saturday's game. Hunt was a foot away from the ball as it came back off the crossbar, and yet he left it, his arm held upright in celebration. It had to be a goal.

One thing is for certain, in all of this did it / didn't it debate. The footballing public are engaged in football in a way they never have been before. I remember Spurs winning the European Cup-Winners Cup in 1963, and finishing second in the First Division the same season. I was just eight years old. There was a fantastic feeling around the place, but nothing like the mood there is now as the nation prepares for its second bite at the World Cup cherry.

If you stop in the baker's for more than ten seconds he'll offer up his opinion about the linesman. The fat lady in the Home and Colonial keeps talking about what a lovely young man that Martin Peters is, how he reminds her of her Graham before he went off to the war. I think she's batty actually, because the photo of her 'Graham' looks more like Jack Charlton than Martin Peters. Still, the point is that they're all talking about football.

On Monday evening I manage to get to seventeen before the ball comes off the top of my knee and skies over the wall into next door's garden. There's a news item on the radio detailing how Jimmy Greaves has been training with the England first team, and the speculation is that Ramsey may well decide to play him tomorrow night.

Would Greaves have seen his shot come back off the bar, or would he have angled his body over it so there was nothing left to chance? Is he a more natural finisher than Hurst? Greaves has always been a striker, after all, long before Hurst even made the West Ham first team. And Hurst came in as a left half before Greenwood moved him up front. Is football all so pre-meditated? It's just a man and a piece of inflated leather, after all. I can't even get the plastic version in a circle twenty times yet, no matter how hard I try.

There's never been a World Cup Final replay before, believe it or not. It's only the second time since the tournament began that there has been extra time. I am wondering if I'll have another dream. I hope not, because I now realise that it ruined the final for me. It's impossible to concentrate on events as they unfold if you have some pre-conception nagging away at the back of your mind.

I haven't told any of my friends about it. Charlie – he's the really good footballer – he'd just laugh. If I was even a quarter as good as him, I'd make it, I know I would. But he doesn't care – football doesn't seem to matter to him – he's always been good at it, he's never really had to think. Like everything in his life. With our eleven plus exams, mum paid for me to have a tutor, and even then I only got into the Grammar on appeal. He sailed through, and was even out playing with his mates on the green the night before the exam. Nothing seems as concentrated in his life, but then perhaps he doesn't really enjoy things like I do.

I first met Charlie playing football, strangely enough. His team were playing with four against the Rowlands' kids from Colindale, and getting hammered. His brother asked me if I wanted to play, so I ran back to the house and got my plimsolls. I didn't make much difference really – it ended up 24-3, or something like that. Charlie scored all our goals. We had ice creams afterwards and I found out he went to Greenview. He was the only one from our team who didn't care about the result.

But then he'd scored the goals, he'd done something in the game. The rest of us had spent most of the two hours running down the hill to fetch the ball after one of theirs had rounded the keeper and tried to send the ball into outer space. They only needed to tap it over the line but, well, maybe it was more fun to have us having to chase after it before it ended up under a lorry in the main road. I got fed up retrieving it in the end and just left it there. No-one else would go, so that was when the game ended. I got it in the end. That was when we had the ice cream. I never did quite find out how we ended up kicking uphill when we were already outnumbered three to one by the opposition. Not a level playing field, in any sense.

I don't have a dream that night. At the breakfast table, dad's reading the paper before going off to work. Normally he's off long before I'm even up for school, but I'm up early today because I can't stop thinking about the final. Dad's a postman, so he needs to be off at half six most days.

'Says here that Ramsey has to play Hurst after Saturday.' I look up at the headline on the back page – 'Hurst will play.' 'Is he scoring a hat-trick tonight, d'you think, Roy?'

I don't offer a reply. My predictions talent has no dream to fire it today.

'Don't tease him, Bill,' mum says. How does she know? I didn't even mention it to her. Dad must have said. So he did take some notice of what I said. He didn't let on at all.

'He would have got three, if they'd given the goal,' I find myself saying.

'You might be right, Roy,' she went on. 'When your confidence is up, sometimes you feel you can do anything – and sometimes, just sometimes, you do.'

I smiled at her. It was just words, but I suddenly felt that this match tonight still might possess something, some magic, that might be going to change my life. We hadn't been in a final before, England. Not even a semi-final. And here it was – our second World Cup Final in four days. And it was a match we could still win – despite everything.

I've been out the back a couple of times this afternoon, but I can't even get to seven with the ball, so I've been reading my comics upstairs, with the radio blaring away downstairs. All they ever play is that song by Chris Farlowe – 'Baby, baby, baby, you're outta ti-i-i-me. I said baby, baby, baby, you're outta ti-i-i-ime …' and on it goes. Greaves must feel like that, a man for whom this day seemed to have been deliberately manufactured – 'the best striker England have ever had' – I know that was part of the reason Ramsey felt so confident about winning the World Cup back when he made that dangerous prediction.

Just as I'm wondering whether Greaves might be training with the other England players, the news comes on at five o'clock. Incredible news. Greaves is playing.

Who has Ramsey left out?

Halfway down the stairs I crash into mum who's coming up to tell me, but she can't remember any of the other names. She knows, as a lifetime member of the Jimmy Greaves appreciation society, that this is the most important news in the house for a long time.

So who has he left out?

I don't know why I should care, but it's now that I realise that Saturday's game has had an odd effect on me, an unexpected effect. I am beginning to offer silent prayers in a gambling game with God – please don't let it be Geoff Hurst that he's dropped. The hat-trick that never was, the goal that never was, they have affected me and the way I'm thinking. I am glad that Greaves is in the team, but I am beginning to feel sick – really sick to the pit of my stomach, that Greaves' inclusion might have been at the expense of Hurst. Hurst, who could not be blamed for the whim of a linesman's decision that denied him a second World Cup Final goal. He got in the shot, he scored the 'goal' – in short, he did enough to be included in tonight's starting eleven.

Ramsey has got cold feet at the last minute, and doesn't want posterity to judge him as The Manager Who Left Out Greaves. I feel he could be making an even bigger mistake, though, if he leaves out Hurst. He can't leave him out. I realise I am in the last days of something profound.

22 days into the tournament, still gripped by World Cup fever.

Can you magic something into happening just through sheer will?

Even if you have no blood connection, no vocational connection, no kind of any connection with the event?

Can I will England to win this game?

Two hours later, and I've digested the news. Ramsey has dropped Hurst, *dropped* him because of that bloody linesman. In the end will it matter years from now – Greaves is as likely to score – maybe more likely, despite his disappointing World Cup record. I just can't help thinking about Geoff Hurst – about his life – he will never have this chance again. To play in a World Cup Final in your own country and to score the winning goal – if England lose, he will feel that fate turned viciously against him in one single sickening moment – of course if they win, there will be other heroes and he will become the forgotten man.

It has been decided that England will wear white in the replay, the Germans wearing their away strip of green shirts and white shorts. Portugal's green socks in the semi-finals, the first vanquished. 'I wanna be in that number, when the whites / reds go marching in ...'

England could have won in red – their away colours – on their home turf – an interesting twist, but tonight they are back in their familiar white and as Greaves runs out, sporting the number 8 shirt, the crowd are stirred up into fits of hyperventilated welcoming cheers, as if he has just scored the winner, welcoming him back for the first time since his untimely injury against France earlier in the tournament.

West Germany have never beaten England – just the two draws, one of them on Saturday – but there's always a first time ... And they're all here at the house now. My granddad, my Uncle Pete and Barry from next door. But there's a different atmosphere, and it has to be Greaves. If he'd played Saturday he might have looked strange in a red shirt, but in the white shirt and blue shorts of England, he could be playing for Spurs.

I look around for Hurst in the warm-up, but there's been no mention of him so far. He must be in the ground somewhere. Does he sit with the team? Greaves was alongside Ramsey on Saturday. What must it have been like to have received the news that you aren't playing even though you scored a World Cup Final goal, even though you should have been credited with a goal which would almost certainly have won the game? 'Gutted' isn't adequate. The worst feeling any sportsman could feel – maybe even worse than realising you've broken your leg in a bad tackle. At least you could damn fate for that, but Ramsey has had a choice here – and although he stuck with him for the final, he hasn't followed through with the sense of premonition his first decision possessed. He has gone for the obvious choice.

The Germans – nobody's really thinking about them or their team, but it has to be as passionate from their end of the telescope. Their heroes, their hopes, their dreams. They've never ever beaten England in an international game, so winning this evening would be something extraordinary for them. In the parallel German household, Willi or Hans or whoever is sitting by his fireplace with his teambook of the players and his hopes and dreams ... A Bayern Munich fan or Munich

1860, or even that other side I was reading about, Eintracht Frankfurt. But the West Germans won the World Cup in 1954, in Switzerland – England had never even got to a semi-final until this year. So we have to win it.

The West Germans are unchanged from Saturday's line-up, so the only difference to the 22 from the game of four days ago is that Greaves steps in for Hurst. Hugh Johns, the commentator, has mentioned the fact that the Russian linesman Tofik Bakhramov has been replaced by a Spanish linesman from a quarter-final match earlier in the tournament. Does that mean he's been subtly censured for his deciding judgement on Hurst's goal? Hardly subtle.

Can the one change make the deciding difference tonight?

The men round the table have arrived in plenty of time and are already two glasses of beer the worse for wear. The fact that it's a night game has seen my digestive biscuit upgraded to a caramel bar, which hardly touches the sides as I wolf it down, my eyes not leaving the screen. England have a corner less than a minute after the kick-off. Ball has gone over to take it. Charlton is up at the far post, but Tilkowski has no problem with the overhit corner.

It seems an age since Saturday, and odd not to see Hurst's toothless grimace at overhit passes or offside decisions. Greaves is an altogether more lithe and compact player who seems to run with the ball barely ahead of him, as if it's being beamed from out of his chest into his path. He has very little backlift, and he moves gracefully, deceptively quickly, with a slight turn, and he's past his man.

He is better than Hurst, no-one can doubt it, but Hurst's silent banishment is still everywhere in my thoughts, even as Greaves accelerates past Beckenbauer, who has been caught horribly out of position. He runs parallel with the edge of the penalty box before hitting a shot on the turn that bobbles on the pitch over the despairing dive of Tilkowski. England are ahead, ahead for the first time since Peters' late goal on Saturday.

Greaves waves a paw at the sky, but there are no histrionics, just a measured walk back to the centre circle. Twelve minutes gone, it's a dream start for England. Hugh Johns' commentary is less excitable than Saturday – '… it's Jim-my Greaves! The Tottenham man scoring a typical Greaves' goal to give England the lead!'

The Germans look weary, and the importance of scoring first in this replay suddenly emerges, ever so slightly, on the faces of the men in the darker shirts. Held, Seeler and Haller, all get shots in over the next quarter of an hour, but only speculatively from outside the box. Cohen and Wilson close up the defence and Bobby Moore lets nothing through. I wonder how he must feel, Moore. It's said that he is mates with Greaves, but Hurst is a team-mate. The events surrounding the team selection must seem bitter sweet in the light of the goal. Even as I'm thinking it, Moore takes a free-kick just inside the England half which Hunt flicks over Weber's head and suddenly Greaves is in again, having crept in on the blind side of the German defence.

'... and Greaves has caught them out, and he takes the ball past Schulz, and he's scored! Greaves has a second in the World Cup Final after just twenty-eight minutes, and the Germans look distraught!'

Johns is right. They have lost whatever it was that kept them in the game until the last minute of normal time on Saturday. Tonight it looks as though England have already got one hand on the cup, even though there is still over an hour of the game left to go.

No-one has mentioned Hurst, and though an imaginative director might have had one of the cameraman search him out from around the England bench, he remains anonymous, just another Englishman in the crowd.

In the dying seconds of the half a charge of a German attack is broken down on the left by a Nobby Stiles' foul. Schnellinger takes the kick short to Emmerich who feigns left to give himself a little space and then chips the ball a full twenty-five yards over the stranded Banks who watches it drop beyond him. It seems an age before the ball lands on the top of the crossbar, bouncing back into the relieved Banks' outstretched hands.

Schnellinger looks on in disbelief, first at the genius of his effort, and then at the cruel end to the moment. England are relieved to go in two ahead, and as perfectly a timed goal it would have been for the Germans, so it proves a commanding indelible line under the England first half performance.

'If only he'd picked him on Saturday, Roy,' dad says, more to the men around him than to me.

'Greavsie's made the difference, Bill, there's no doubt about it,' Uncle Pete purrs, mawkishly. I can't remember Uncle Pete ever saying anything controversial, anything to challenge the mood of what's around us. Like the nodding dog in the back of our car, he only ever agrees with what's being said.

I want to make a case for Hurst, to talk about the hat-trick that should have been, but whilst the choice of angry emotive words to make the case jumbles to a selective finish in my head, I just sit there silent, looking ahead at the screen, at the marching display by the Massed Bands of Her Majesty's Royal Marines, all strutting their military stuff. Who was it who dreamed up military music for half-time entertainment at a football match? What has it got to do with football? And no-one ever questions it. They get them at Spurs, too. Marching up and down the pitch so the ball is even harder for the players to control in the second half.

Mum pushes another cup of tea at me – and two more caramel biscuits.

England are out for the second half, a lot more eager than West Germany. They make another storming raid down Germany's right flank in the persons of Ball and Peters, the latter curling in a perfectly weighted cross that Greaves meets at the far post. His header down heads for the corner of Tilkowski's goal, but the keeper makes an astonishing save, flicking it away. On any other day, it might have been a moment to inspire the Germans, but Hunt is too quick, and snatches at the loose ball to kick it high into the goal beyond the stranded last defender. 3-0.

'And if anyone has any doubts about Alf Ramsey's prediction now, we're not going to be hearing them above this noise…' Johns' gleeful tones of excitement perfectly capture the roar, and Hunt points up into the crowd at someone important to him – we hear later that it was his wife.

Then, on the hour, the Germans pull one back – England are knocking the ball around a little too casually, and almost like a move in a Rugby match, Overath intercepts a lazy square pass from Bobby Charlton, who's had a quiet game, and hares down on Banks' goal, clipping the ball over him as the Leicester keeper meets him at the edge of the penalty area.

This time the ball escapes the spell that England, and in particular Greaves, seems to have on it tonight under the Wembley floodlights. Odd that Moore will be winning his third Wembley trophy in successive years, each one an improvement on the previous effort. Last year West Ham won the European Cup Winners Cup, two years after Spurs, under the Wembley floodlights. Tonight, well, tonight it's us, it's England. For the first time ever.

I couldn't appreciate it four years ago – I was only eight – the moment Greaves tried to grab that dog in the game against Brazil and it weed all over his shirt – England falling at the Quarter-Final stage –

I didn't really understand disappointment then – but this year I do, and I also understand the peculiar joy, the unique pleasure of sitting on the top of the football pile.

I think I see Hurst for a moment, but it isn't him, just a rabid supporter, smiling a toothless grin. And Greaves hasn't finished yet. For the criticism that says he isn't a team player, Greaves almost embraces it with a solo run from the end of the centre circle, the orange ball a blur under his feet, taking Beckenbauer with him, before blasting a low shot past Tilkowski for England's fourth.

This time the celebrations are ones of ecstasy, for Greaves has achieved what Hurst was denied on Saturday, a hat-trick in a World Cup Final, the first ever in the history of the tournament.

At the other end, with a quarter of an hour left, Seeler heads a second for Germany from a corner, but the celebrations are beginning. The cameras run over the giant scoreboard whose dwarfing letters pronounce England 4 W Germany 2 ...

The cameramen seem to be more interested in the crowd than following the game, and a shot of a group of girls twirling their rattles hangs on the screen for an age before the picture cuts back to a Bobby Charlton thunderbolt which strikes the referee on the shoulder before spooning in the air away for a goal kick.

England try to press home their advantage when of all people George Cohen makes a rare run into the German defence and plays a one-two with Roger Hunt to find himself straight through on goal, and although Schulz gets in a tackle, the ball runs loose to Greaves who sweeps it inches wide with the goal at his mercy. And then ... possibly the euphoria of the final whistle, but probably a simple rush of blood to the head, and Hugh Johns lets out words that will sum up the moment for decades to come, '... and that's it, the war's finally over – the Germans will have to surrender now!'

Uncle Pete and Barry think it's hilarious. Mum thinks it's in bad taste.

'That stupid man,' she says. 'It's only a game of football. How could he say that?'

Dad keeps his counsel, but her comments have subdued the developing party in the front room. I've soon forgotten the words, and instead watch Bobby Moore and Gordon Banks climbing the stairs to collect their medals. Jimmy Greaves resists Nobby Stiles and Martin Peters' efforts to lift him up in a sequence that will be replicated in photo montages up and down the years ahead. He has scored three goals in a World Cup Final that seemed to have eluded him just four days earlier.

It's a feat that is unlikely ever to be repeated in the life of the modern game. Greaves doesn't seem particularly elated, not even surprised. He did score four against Norway back in June in a friendly, but this is The World Cup Final! Jimmy Greaves is destined to become the most famous footballer in the world, and even in his quiet, measured strides on the lap of honour around the running track at Wembley, he knows something has changed forever.

I'm not particularly interested in Greaves at this point, though the taste of victory is everywhere. I'm looking round the lines on the television for a sense of what the tournament has been all about, for the defining moment. It's not Bobby Moore, not Nobby Stiles, not even Jimmy Greaves.

And finally I see him, a small figure behind Alf Ramsey who is talking broken English with the German manager. Geoff Hurst. He is there as a shape against the skyline, but he doesn't make any of the photographs adorning the newspapers over the following weeks. There are no interviews with him on radio or television. Nothing is said about that disputed disallowed goal in the eleventh minute of extra time on Saturday July 30th 1966. What could have meant so much, now means nothing.

His life, along with mine, will never be the same again.

CHAPTER TWO

The End of the Sixties

I am about to sit my examinations, but my studies, as they have become known in this house, are not going very well. It shouldn't make much difference, as I got through the mock exams okay, but unless I've spent three hours in my room with my head in a text book then I might as well not bother expecting anything on my plate for tea.

How can any of them eat anything in this house? Not that they've had to suffer the shame of seeing their team relegated from the best football league in the world.

I suppose I ought to explain for any of you that don't follow West Ham, just what's gone on since the Greatest Day in English Football. Don't get me wrong, winning the World Cup was a truly exhilarating experience. It's just that events closest to a football fan's heart are usually more domestically inclined.

For Jimmy Greaves, Sir Jimmy Greaves, any day after 2nd August 1966 was just another day as the Greatest Striker in the History of the Game. The achievements continued to pile up: top scorer for Spurs 1966-67 with 41 goals, another ten up until Christmas 1968, then the transfer to Manchester United. The 'Dream Team' partnership with – take your pick – any one of Brian Kidd, Denis Law or George Best. Then there was Greaves' fiftieth England Goal, coming as it did in his 88th international. I should have shared in the joy felt by all the members of this house, but something unexpected happened to me on that day back in August 1966.

Geoff Hurst happened.

I couldn't get that vision of the forgotten man out of my mind throughout the summer. His bludgeoned expression and tourniqueted fate had rendered my disposition as a football supporter permanently damaged. And so I did the unthinkable. I became a West Ham United fan.

I hadn't exactly made a bargaining tool of my football allegiance, but I suppose my dad thought, after all those times he had taken me to White Hart Lane, that I would become a Spurs supporter – like the last three generations of our family. But I didn't.

I couldn't.

The Press had been overwhelmingly generous in their praise of the England coach, Sir Alf Ramsey, forgiving him for his 'mistake' of selecting Hurst with a fit Jimmy Greaves available on the bench, but there was always an undercurrent of lurking criticism, ready to flood out at any moment. Hurst hasn't played for England since, but now, as we prepare to defend the Jules Rimet Trophy in Mexico, something tells me nothing less than a second successive tournament win will keep Ramsey from getting the sack. And the way things are with the England team at the moment, he might as well start making sure he's sorted out his pension.

So I became a West Ham United fan. Bubbles. The Irons. Fortune's always hiding, and all that. The first time I went to the Boleyn I could only wonder why I'd never been before. The crowd seemed more patient, more knowledgeable than the White Hart Lane mob. Then there was the humour, the irony and the phlegmatism in defeat. And there were plenty of opportunities for that after the summer of 1966.

With the captain of the World Champions in your team, it was assumed that the Hammers' first season after the World Cup would be profitable. Out of the League and FA Cups at the first time of asking, their League form wasn't much better, and but for the ineptness of Blackpool and Aston Villa, Hammers would certainly have been relegated.

Somehow our achievements – or lack of them – didn't bother me that season. The fact that we were there, in the First Division, was all that mattered. I had made a statement in the house, albeit a small one, that I was an individual and that my choice of football team wasn't to be taken for granted. It was like a funeral when Spurs lost out to Manchester United on goal difference at the end of the season – no-one seemed to notice that Hammers had only managed survival by a point. Dad even said that point was wasted on keeping West Ham up when it could have meant the title going to Spurs for the first time since 1961.

And so it went on for the next few years. In 1967-68 Hammers managed to get to the semi-finals of the FA Cup thanks to three goals each from Dear and Heffer, though that wasn't why we were called 'animals' in the 1-0 defeat at Old Trafford against Burnley. The double sending-off of Billy Bonds and Harry Redknapp – two inexperienced players contesting the award of a ludicrous penalty for a foul by Bonds on Ralph Coates, didn't help matters. In the league seventeenth was better than twentieth, but not much better. It was also believed that Bobby Moore had handed in a transfer request to Ron Greenwood. He'd rejected it of course, but the gesture was almost as bad as him going.

In 1968-69, Hammers were again saved by the poor form of two other struggling sides, Leicester City and Queens Park Rangers, and again finished twentieth, missing out on relegation by three points. Martin Peters left the side in the summer to join Tottenham – much to dad's delight – but for some reason Bobby Moore stayed, as did a new emerging talent, Trevor Brooking.

So to this season, and the unthinkable – relegation after just twelve years back in the First Division. It wasn't exactly a surprise for the form – or lack of it – shown since 1966, but it has still been a really tough cross to bear, and in my O'Level year, too. The only thing that even makes it halfway bearable, is that Arsenal were relegated alongside us, despite their so-called international forward line. So how is it that we are going down to the Second Division, just weeks before the 1970 World Cup? And how come they haven't sacked Ron Greenwood?

There are other things in my life apart from football. Well, apart from West Ham, I should say. Practising out with that ball in the back yard must have paid off, as I've kept my place as a wing back in the school team for the last four years. Added to that, even though I'm only just sixteen, I played the last three games of the season in the school First XI.

Dad was good at sport; he played cricket and football for the first army battalion team in the war, but he never managed to get into the school football First XI. It's true that he left school at sixteen, but he wasn't a regular in any of the teams in his time there. He's taken some interest in my progress, but he's often too busy on a Saturday morning. He has to catch up on his sleep, and rarely gets up before one, by which time I'm back from the game and am already out in the afternoon up in town with my mates.

Then again something happened when I chose not to support Spurs. It was as though I was making a decision to leave home and live somewhere else. Dad stopped talking to me about football. He'd talk about England's performances, but even then it was 'That Bobby Moore of yours,' or 'No wonder Martin Peters saw sense and came to Tottenham.'

I've given up trying to win him back – I'm just letting him get on with it. I'm still pleased when Spurs win (so long as it's not against West Ham) but I don't bother telling him any more. He wouldn't believe me, anyway.

One thing – at least he hasn't been laughing about Hammers getting relegated. Just as well. I suppose he's put himself in my shoes and imagined what it might be like if Spurs were to go down. Not that they will now, with the team that they've got. People already talking about them winning the league next year, even without Jimmy Greaves.

So – just how could we get relegated with the England captain at the helm? I suppose you have to go back to the beginning of the season to start explaining that.

It wasn't as though we'd been challenging for the title since the World Cup. Three seasons of indifferent form – any one of which could have seen us in the Second Division – but no investment in the kind of players – goalscorers for example – that might have made a difference and helped us to start climbing up the table. Then we lost Martin Peters – I suppose that was the last straw.

We started well enough, winning the two opening games 1-0, both at home, against Newcastle and Chelsea. Hurst scored both the goals, and despite his rather unkempt beard, he actually looked quite sharp in front of goal. Those two games flattered the team, as we lost the next three. One of those was a crazy game at Chelsea, who'd just had a set of ludicrous new floodlights fitted. It was like the fitters had forgotten to tighten the screws or something, and the lights danced across the pitch throughout the game, which we lost 3-0 thanks to a hat-trick from the flashy feet of Peter Osgood.

I travel to most of these games with Charlie Barth, my talented mate from the First XI who's already on Crystal Palace's books. He's a striker who lives in Colindale, so it's odd that Palace picked him up, but that's football I suppose. He can get free tickets for the Palace games, but more about that later.

So after a 2-2 draw against Arsenal and a goal apiece for new striking partners of Roger Cross and Bermudian midweek signing Clyde

Best, the real nightmare run began. Ten successive defeats. There's nothing ambiguous about that. On the surface there appeared to be no real explanation for the slump – West Ham's worse for over two decades – apart perhaps from Clyde Best's hamstring injury against Tottenham in only his third game. Greenwood tries everything he can, playing Roger Cross, Geoff Hurst and even Paul Heffer up front. The goals dry up and the run looks like this:

Nottingham Forest (a)	0-1
Tottenham Hotspur (h)	0-1
Everton (a)	0-2
Sheffield Wednesday (h)	0-2
Manchester United (a)	0-6
Burnley (h)	0-1
Stoke City (h)	1-3
Coventry City (a)	0-2
Wolverhampton (a)	0-1
Sunderland (h)	0-1

Even the 'goal' against Stoke City was an own goal, scored by Terry Conroy. That's an incredible run – ten straight league defeats. It was actually, strictly speaking, eleven, as we lost to Nottingham Forest in the League Cup too, a month after losing to them in the league.

Can the finger be pointed at anyone in particular? Where do you start? Well let's start with the goalkeeper. Bobby Ferguson. You can't even call him butter fingers, as butter would be too expensive for him. Margerine Mitts, Charlie called him, after he dropped an Alan Ball corner into his own net against Everton. He has quite a powerful goal kick, which would be handy if he could kick the ball straight. He often reminds me of a rugby full back kicking for touch, that's how wayward his clearances are.

What about the defence? It's hard to blame Billy Bonds for anything – he's one of the few players who manages to play with guts and with his heart on his sleeve. The fans love that. Then again, he was booked four times in that ten game run, so much so that he faced an FA disciplinary enquiry. Frank Lampard came back after a broken leg, but doesn't seem to be half the player, darting out of tackles. He's lost a yard of pace, too. John Charles 'disappeared' in too many of those ten games, as did Bobby Howe. Bobby Moore has all the grandeur you'd expect on the ball, but you have to feel some sympathy for him when he gathers possession on the edge of the West Ham penalty area. It's as though he hasn't got a single person to pass to, for fear that they'll give the ball away too easily.

Ronnie Boyce has been in and out, but the best days of his career are over. As for Alan Stephenson, last year's hero has become a nervous wreck – the fans have recently been given to cheering whenever he completes an accurate pass. I know I shouldn't say it, but Charlie could get in that West Ham team easily. He's got a fantastic left foot, and scored twenty-one goals for the Palace under-18s this season. If he was on West Ham's books he'd probably already be playing for the reserves. But he isn't, and if I can only think of one thing worse than the season it's been watching West Ham, it'd be watching their reserve team.

At least the run of defeats finally came to an end, with a draw at Southampton, the only side, it seemed, ready to compete with us for the First Division's wooden spoon. No one in the ground looked more surprised than Trevor Brooking when he put the Hammers ahead with a tap in after Terry Paine fell over, unchallenged, in the penalty area. Unfortunately West Ham completed the Comedy of Errors when Mick Channon was let in to equalise at the end.

Why do we keep going to watch our team when they're playing like that? Perhaps these are the times that show who the real fans are. Upton Park was the first place I ever heard the word 'masochist' spoken. 'I must be a bloody masochist,' one bloke said, so I looked it up when I got home, anticipating the definition: West Ham Football Supporter. *Deriving pleasure from pain*, I read. It didn't seem right. There was very little pleasure to be had at the Boleyn Ground this season, or any of the previous three, to be honest, so it was hard to understand what the man at the ground must have meant.

Hammers were bottom of the league at the beginning of November with just six points from a possible 34, and just two wins in their 17 games. Despite grabbing odd points here and there and a further six wins, their finishing total of twenty points was their worst ever in any division. Even before they played Crystal Palace (a game Charlie got us into free), West Ham were already relegated.

The fans were incredible, cheering every goal and giving the side as much support as they could, even during that miserable run in September and October. The home attendances rarely dropped below 25,000, and they took nearly 12,000 fans to the last game away to Arsenal which they won 1-0 against the odds, thanks to a goal from youngster Pat Holland. This support probably had more to do with the fact that Arsenal needed a point to stay up, but it showed just how valuable the fans can be, and in a frenzied noise that sounded like the best of times back at Upton Park, West Ham dragged Arsenal down with them. I am ashamed to admit that it was the highlight of the season for me.

	P	W	D	L	F	A	Pts
19 Crystal Pal	42	6	17	19	46	67	29
20 Southampton	42	6	15	21	34	68	27
21 Arsenal	42	6	14	22	30	68	26
22 West Ham	42	8	4	30	25	61	20

Now we await the World Cup, and my fear is, every time I open dad's paper, that we'll hear how Bobby Moore has gone to Everton or Leeds. It just seems hard to imagine him playing Second Division football next season.

My life's beginning to change in more ways than involuntarily becoming the supporter of a Second Division team. While Hammers have gone down, my own fortunes have stopped hiding and are beginning to parade nakedly down the high street. There's something about the 1970s that seems different to anything I can remember in my life before. Charlie's girlfriend Hanna introduced me to her mate Chloe Shrimpton a couple of weeks ago and, well, maybe that's the reason the relegation hasn't hit quite as hard as I thought it might.

Going to a boys' school, you get used to all these foul smells – sweat, bad breath, farting and kids who don't wash – and then this girl, Chloe. Well that was the first thing I noticed about her. How sweet she smells. Her hair is always like she's just washed it ten minutes earlier – her breath is like she's crammed four packets of parma violets down her throat on her way to meet me – and her skin is like a baby's – like my little sister's skin. I just want to get close to it and smell it all the time. Which I'm sure makes me appear like some kind of perve, but when something smells that beautiful – well, you've just got to smell it.

I'm not quite sure what she sees in me – but when I'm competing with that, you can bet that I've just crammed six packets of parma violets down my throat, that I've just washed my hair and that I haven't long got out of the bath before I meet up with her.

We haven't done anything yet – not serious – but that's coming, I know. She's really mature in the way she behaves when we are alone, even though that doesn't happen much because of her mum. This is on account of the fact that her mum's sister is this big time model who's always off to Paris and New York, and who's told her things about men that seem to have put her off them for life. Her mum's divorced, of course, so she probably hates men just for the hell of it. Then again, Chloe's dad was an Arsenal fan, so her mum must have some sense. Imagine being married to someone who couldn't stop going on about Charlie George and John Radford. You'd have to divorce them in the end, wouldn't you?

Anyway, so that's happening, and then Charlie's knocking on the door of the reserves at Palace, and has promised me he'll get me a trial there early next season. Of course I'd rather be at Chadwell Heath donning the claret and blue, but then beggars can't be choosers, and Palace are still in the First Division – just.

So, yeah, the seventies. Well, the first six months of them, anyway. Apart from West Ham slipping out of the First Division, this isn't too bad a place to be at the moment. The World Cup is just around the corner, and as we are the holders, there's plenty of optimism about our chances of retaining the trophy, even though no European side has ever won the tournament outside of Europe.

As holders we qualify without playing a match, and here's the squad: England's squad: Goalkeepers: Gordon Banks (Stoke City), Peter Bonetti (Chelsea), Alex Stepney (Manchester United); Defenders: Keith Newton (Everton), Terry Cooper (Leeds United), Alan Mullery (Crystal Palace), Brian Labone (Everton), Bobby Moore (West Ham United), Tommy Wright (Everton), Jackie Charlton (Leeds United), Norman Hunter (Manchester City); Midfielders: Francis Lee (Manchester City), Alan Ball (Blackpool), Martin Peters (Tottenham Hotspur), Nobby Stiles (Manchester United), Emlyn Hughes (Blackpool), Colin Bell (Manchester City); Forwards: Bobby Charlton (Manchester United), Jimmy Greaves (Manchester United), Peter Osgood (Chelsea), Joe Royle (Everton), Jeff Astle (West Bromwich Albion). Coach: Sir Alf Ramsey.

Sir Matt Busby should be managing the team bearing in mind half of it is from Manchester United, but people generally reckon we've got half a chance, even though we are in a group with the favourites Brazil. Might as well get them out of the way as early as possible so far as I can see.

I've been trying to persuade dad to buy a new television in time for the tournament, but he seems happy with the one we watched the 1966 World Cup on.

'It may be old, but it's paid for,' is his mantra. He's still working for the Post Office, which is one reason why we have a phone in every room, even though only one of them rings out. I still have to go down the road to the phone box whenever I want to ring Chloe. No chance that dad could end up working for a company making televisions so we could have one of them in every room. Charlie's parents, of course, have a colour TV, so it looks as though that's where I'll be watching most of the games. This is, of course, always supposing that dad lets me over there, bearing in mind half of the games take place in the middle of the night.

None of these arguments would have half the sting they seem to possess if I could have the exams under my belt and be back at school. The trouble is that they don't start until next week and then I have to wait until the end of August before I can get my hand on the results. I have to do well – I have to get at least six out of the eight if I want to go back to the sixth form next September. Dad's already lining me up for a job in the Post Office if I don't get the necessary qualifications.

Two weeks on and I'm in the middle of it all. Charlie's been offered a contract at Crystal Palace and he and his parents have a meeting with Bert Head next week. I'm over halfway through the exams which seem to be going fine, unlike the world of football.

Ron Greenwood and Bobby Moore have had a falling out over Moore's transfer request. All the top clubs are lining up to buy him, which hasn't exactly been helping England's prospects, defending the World Cup in Mexico. They managed to win their group, despite losing to Brazil, and are playing Peru in the quarter-finals tomorrow – Sunday June 14th. This is only because Brazil somehow lost to Romania when all they had to do was draw to win the group. This was in no small part due to the tactics of the Romanians, who crocked Pele in the first ten minutes in an Eastern European sandwich that means he may well miss the rest of the tournament. Pretty ironic when he said after 1966 that he would never play again as a result of the tackling he was subjected to – he must be regretting his change of heart.

As far as England are concerned, while Moore and Greenwood were bashing each other over the phone and quite publicly in the press prior to the tournament, Jimmy Greaves was accused of stealing a kid's pink romper suit from a tourist shop in Colombia. This wasn't that easy to explain seeing as he was in the shop with Alan Ball, who – sizewise, anyway – he could have been argued to have been stealing it for. Thankfully the British Consulate get involved and everything is cleared up. I'm not sure that doesn't influence disciplinarian Ramsey's decision to use Greaves as a substitute, even though he's still only thirty, for the opening game against Romania. With ten minutes to go, and England struggling to hold the Romanians at 0-0, super-sub Greavsie comes on and scores a couple. Even though we lose 1-0 to Brazil, Crystal Palace's Alan Mullery scores the winner from midfield against Czechoslovakia, and we're in the quarter-finals on goal difference.

England 2-0 Romania
Brazil 2-1 Czechoslovakia
Romania 1-1 Czechoslovakia
Brazil 1-0 England
Brazil 2-3 Romania
England 1-0 Czechoslovakia

Final Group G table

	P	W	D	L	F	A	Pts
England	3	2	0	1	3	1	4
Brazil	3	2	0	1	5	4	4
Romania	3	1	1	2	4	5	3
Czechoslovakia	3	0	1	2	2	4	1

If we can beat Peru, we'll play the winner of the Uruguay v Soviet Union quarter-final. If West Germany, who've done well to win their group, can win their quarter and semi-finals (though that would involve beating Brazil!) we might even be involved in a repeat of the 1966 World Cup Final. Then again, we're hardly going to worry about the Germans, who've never beaten us before, and aren't about to use this World Cup tournament to start a run of victories against us.

There's been an article about Geoff Hurst who, despite his best season at West Ham for four years – that's not saying much, though at least he got into double figures with his goal tally, 10 – has apparently been suffering in his role as the 'forgotten man' since the 1966 tournament. The *Daily Mail* has been writing about his fall from grace, from a scorer in a World Cup Final, to a Second Division player, shunned by England since that game four years ago. There have even been rumours of a drink problem building up over the last eighteen months. As a fan, I don't need much persuasion to believe that there might be some truth in these stories. Rather strangely, though, Hurst does not go public with any kind of statement to strengthen or repudiate these accusations. Affording a lawyer might be an issue on a Second Division player's wages, but then the best way to answer his critics would be to lose a bit of weight and start knocking them in to get West Ham back in the top flight at the first time of asking.

Charlie has decided to sign for Palace — no big surprise there — which means he doesn't really have to bother about his exams. I don't think he was really bothered about them anyway, to tell you the truth, but it's a happy ending for him. These days, players can make their debuts for clubs at seventeen, and he's seventeen next November. He's promised to get me a trial at Selhurst Park, though I'm not holding my breath.

The exams are over, and I think I've done okay, which is pretty much what was expected. I'd love to end up playing football for a living, but I've read the stories. Even if you sign up with a club, the chances of making it even into the first team are less than one in fifty. For any kind of success in the game, you're talking one in a thousand. I'm not a gambler, though I suppose I can dream ... and if my mate is at a First Division club, then at least I'll know what it might be like to have the chance.

Charlie and I have become really good mates over the summer break. Weird how we won't be together next September for the first time in five years. Imagine going to a football training ground every day of your life — for a job. It hardly seems credible. And footballers are always portrayed as being somehow thick — it's like their brains ended up in their feet, so that's why they had to leave school. Well there's nothing thick about Charlie — he's better than me in the Sciences and History — and he'll probably get all eight of his O'Levels, whether he needs them or not.

Last Sunday afternoon we watched England play Peru, in colour, on his dad's telly. It's so different seeing the game in colour. The different shades of green on the pitch, the black of the referee's outfit — he's the only one in black looking at it this way. Then there is the sweat on the players' faces, the brown of the mud as the pitch breaks up, and the crimson of the blood from injuries. Not only that, but the way the game is covered is so different. It's not just the commentator and his summariser, there's a whole studio of football analysts, panellists and slow-motion replays to solve any disputes. This doesn't actually work though, because often the 'evidence' ends up allowing other theories to be concocted as to why something happened. Case in point, the Romanians, who have been trying to claim that Pele manufactured the event to sit out the rest of the game so that Brazil would finish second and avoid having to go head-to-head in the quarter-finals with Peru, a fellow South American team, that they preferred to meet in the final. Strangely the replay of the incident raised even more doubts about the incident than it put to bed.

Peru was the country Bobby Moore made his debut against in a friendly back in 1962 which got us all excited about our chances. They were managed by Didi, one of the greatest ever Brazilian players, so there was never any doubt as to how his team would play. With Peru and their red diagonal striped tops, England were in their first team white shirts – so they would actually have looked the same on a black and white television (as my dad later remarked). Ramsey started with an attacking formation, playing Greaves up front with Joe Royle and Bobby Charlton. Jimmy Hill, back in the ITV studios (Charlie's dad also preferred ITV over BBC) remarked after the goalless first half that it wasn't working precisely because Royle and Greaves were the same kind of player and were cancelling each other out. It was like playing with ten men.

It wasn't the game I was watching. England had been unlucky, with Royle's miskick in front of goal after ten minutes and Bobby Charlton's twenty-five yard dipping volley that had clipped the crossbar with the keeper beaten. Peru's chances had been limited, although the amount of possession they'd had in the game made it hard to believe that they'd only managed a header straight at Bonetti (Banks was out of the side with food poisoning) and a long shot from the Teófilo Cubillas, their most dangerous player.

Dad had been invited to come round and watch the game with me, but had decided not to as a result of what looked to me like a predictable case of terminal pride. I felt bad having to lie and say my granddad was coming over to watch the game there, especially when Charlie's dad said to bring him over too. Charlie smiled at me – he knew my dad, and knew what was going on.

The second half was forty-five minutes of football that people still talk about today. With twenty minutes to go and the game still goalless, Alf Ramsey took off Bobby Charlton and brought on Jeff Astle. That in itself strangely seemed to take the heart out of the England side and their ability to hit Peru on the break, and five minutes before the end, with extra time beckoning, Héctor Chumpitaz broke free after a mistake by Keith Newton who trod on the ball when trying to pass back to Bonetti. Instead of whacking the ball into the stands, Bonetti attempted to take the loose ball past Chumpitaz, lost possession, and the Peruvian calmly stroked it into the net to give the Peruvians the lead. England had nothing left and spent the last five minutes camped out in their own penalty area trying to restrict Peru from scoring a second.

It doesn't get any worse as a fan. Your team relegated from the First Division, and your country out of the World Cup at the hands of a team who were there for only the second time in their history.

I didn't feel like hanging around at Charlie's to hear Jimmy Hill harp on about Ramsey's shortcomings as a manager – even in colour – but couldn't bear the thought of going home to argue with dad, so I went round to Chloe's. It was odd, as I only ever went round there by invitation, keen not to damage my reputation in her mum's eyes, such as it was. I had no intention of screwing up my relationship with Chloe, which was going very nicely, but I felt so miserable about losing to Peru in that way. It was the first time I'd seen England eliminated from a World Cup competition live on television like that, and I hadn't really thought about how I was going to react. The thing about times like these is that you know it's a moment in history in the making, and in that moment you're torn between wanting to write it all down and wanting to do something completely reckless so that what you've done becomes an additional feature of the moment's tapestry.

'Roy? You didn't ring,' she said, opening the door. But she was smiling.
'The football,' I said.
'We were watching.'
'I thought you didn't like football.'
'But it's England.'
She beckoned me inside with a wave of her hand that seemed almost comic, like she was taking me through to a pool party in the garden. Through the dark house with the dying embers of a recent Sunday lunch. It didn't seem quite so ridiculous when she led me through to the conservatory at the back, past the second colour television I'd seen that day. No football this time, just Morecambe and Wise in a routine of face slapping and loud insults.
'Where's …?'

'She's out. Gone to my aunt's for the evening. My nan was round, but she got tired and went home.'

'Shame,' I said.

In my stupor, I tried to gather my thoughts to work out exactly what Chloe was doing. I was still holding her hand, stepping out onto the paved area at the back . Of course – she was pulling out a couple of blankets to put across the sun lounger in the garden. A half finished orange drink was perched on a small metal table at the side of the lounger. I suddenly took in that she was in her bare feet, wearing only a bikini. How had I missed that at the door?

I'd only ever been round her house to call for her in the five weeks since we'd been going out. I'd never been inside. And now the adults were away …

But I had to ask the question.

'When's she back?'

'Don't worry,' Chloe said. The confident speed of her answer and her cool hand on my shoulder had the blood draining from my face and heading south.

Thank God for parma violets and personal cleanliness. I'd heard so many stories about the dangers of failing to observe the scout motto, but this afternoon – evening, as it now was – I opened my eyes as I kissed her and noticed that it had got dark since we'd been out there on the lounger.

Kissing seems so pointless when you're very young; you murmur 'Yeeuurgh!' when you see them do it in old films. Especially with all the family huddled round the television.

Now it seemed so different, so – perfect. I was trying not to breathe, not to spoil it as her mouth hung over mine, her tongue arched into a tiny spear weaving its way to the back of my throat, her lips closing round mine in a move that even Bobby Moore would have had to admire.

How odd that it was supposed to be the bloke who got things moving. It was her hand pulling mine across her top. The way things were taking shape – if you get my meaning – all I'd have to do was lie there and let her organise everything.

It happened so fast – her breasts were out and I was underneath them, trying to look out from under them, suddenly conscious of any well-wishers who might be looking over the fence from next door.

'They're out,' she said.

36

I managed to stop myself laughing by pressing my face into the orb, obligingly suspended within reach of my lips.

'Both sides.'

I didn't know whether she meant the neighbours or the breasts, but things had developed sufficiently for it not to matter. This was what life was all about after football. Defeat was momentary. There would always be another tournament, another season. We'd remember all the conquests and the defeats, but there'd always be another chance to go out and slay the dragon. Another bunch of names fighting the same cause with the same goal in mind.

But nothing could reduce the power of each moment, win or lose. The thing about times like these is that you know it's a moment in history in the making, and in that moment you're torn between wanting to write it all down and wanting to do something completely reckless so that what you've done becomes an additional feature of the moment's tapestry.

And that was exactly what happened that night. I lost my virginity the day England were booted out of the 1970 World Cup by lowly unfancied Peru.

CHAPTER THREE

A Foot Up

The first part of the 1970-71 season was a 'steadying the ship' affair both for West Ham and for me. With the O-Level results in the bag, and dad speaking to me again, the decision to stay on at school was an easy one to make. Far from it being a decisive moment in my life, I saw it as another part in the procrastination jigsaw while I worked out what was really going to happen.

Charlie was already in Crystal Palace reserves, and had even scored a couple of goals in an FA Youth Cup tie in early October at Nottingham Forest when he had been drafted in as the replacement centre forward. I had been up there to watch him, and got talking to Tony Taylor, the Palace first team right half, who said they usually had two open days at the club over Christmas – by invitation – and that I should come down then.

Although I had often dreamed of the glamour of being a striker, I had always played in front of the defence as a wing half, or what some clubs now preferred to call midfield. That and left back for the school from my first two years there. I was now playing regularly for the First XI, in the number 8 shirt. We played in blue shirts with white collars, white shorts and red socks, also Glasgow Rangers' colours. Musn't grumble.

Despite the quality of Grammar School football in England, the games weren't attended by scouts, just a collection of Oxbridge cast out sports masters, all abandoned dreams and resentful attitudes. To succeed in the real game, the beautiful game, you needed a foot up. That foot up would be coming my way a lot sooner than I could have expected.

In the meantime West Ham were getting used to a week-in week-out fixture list that looked like a nineteenth century music hall line-up. It wasn't unpleasant to cross London to visit sides that had been relegated in the past few years like Fulham, but newly promoted Leyton Orient were supposed to be a Hammers' fan's second team, not a team that they actually had to turn up to play on a Saturday, let alone drop points to.

Things had not started too well for the club. Bobby Moore had kept his word and was an international captain playing far from the big league. It was understood that he would only give it one year, which was looking to have been an error of judgement on his part after the first fifteen games. West Ham had won only six of these, and though they had drawn seven, September defeats at Leicester City and Sheffield United had led to calls for Ron Greenwood's head.

The poor man had often been given the title of the 'behind the scenes' architect of England's successful 1966 World Cup campaign and had also often found the blame for Geoff Hurst's drastic loss of form and Martin Peters' 1969 departure from the club resting solely on his shoulders. Greenwood had somehow managed to persuade Bobby Moore to stay after taking the side down, even though Roger Cross had followed Peters to Spurs, but he had failed to lure any big name players to the squad. There would have to be some major improvement in form if he was to remain at the club beyond Christmas.

Roger Morgan, the player who came to Upton Park with £100,000 in exchange for Martin Peters back in May 1969, is currently one of the few bright spots about the club. He has made the majority of the goals scored since he's been at Upton Park – even in the relegation season – and regularly links up well with Trevor Brooking to keep the football entertaining. He's popular with the fans too, with his darting runs and hanging crosses.

It is odd that relegation doesn't seem to have affected the size of the crowds as much as I thought it would – there were over 34,000 for the visit of Arsenal – who look to be going straight back up. They are already nine points clear at the top, and though we managed a draw at Upton Park, the fact that they managed to keep Radford and Kennedy has preserved their goalscoring power.

The irritating thing is that despite being relegated, I still find myself with an interest in the league that we aren't now a part of – the First Division. It's the first time we've been outside it since the 1957-58 season. How galling it must be for Bobby Moore to see the rest of his England colleagues slugging it out week after week in the best Football League in the world. So far this season, Wolves look like they might bring the championship back to Molineux for the first time since 1958-59, West Ham's first season there in the fifties. Bobby Gould, Kenny Hibbitt, Jim McCalliog and John Richards are all playing the season of their lives, along with Peter Knowles, the 25-year-old England inside forward.

It's December 1970, a month in my life that I will never forget for two very different reasons. The first of these is that I've set myself up for that promised trial at Crystal Palace. My dad has already received a letter signed by Bert Head inviting me to attend at the training ground on 28th December at 10am. He's made it clear that there will be thirty other 'hopefuls' there, who will be participating in various activities during the day as well as a knock-out competition in the afternoon. Of course it's all down to Charlie, though he denies it. Our sports master from school Mr Greengate phoned my dad to tell him that the Palace scouts had been at a couple of our games – dad apparently knew on the morning of the second game but still didn't tell me, imagining it would 'put me off' – and one of the games in particular against Cardinal Vaughan school went very well for me, so I wasn't short of luck around that time.

Before any of that could happen, on Monday 7th December 1970, I came home early that afternoon from school, and my mother gave me the news as I opened the door.

'They've sacked Ron Greenwood, Roy. It's been on the radio most of the afternoon.' My face must have been a picture. 'You said they would – and you were right.'

I wondered at the accuracy of my own prediction before replying.

'But mum, this is Ron Greenwood. They didn't even give him a season to get the side back in the First Division.'

Hammers were mid-table in Division Two. I must have realised that it was coming, but it still felt hard to grasp the idea as real. I wandered upstairs, my thoughts jumbled, dropping my bag off in my room. A colour picture of Greenwood was strategically positioned to the left of my '*Shoot* League Tables' which still had early November's positions. I hadn't changed them – I was never too quick to move the teams when West Ham's movement in the table was in line with gravity.

They won the European Cup-Winners Cup under this man, I was thinking. And the FA Cup before that – Greenwood's West Ham team had provided three members of England's World Cup Winning squad – all of them nurtured under the excellent tutelage of the ex-Chelsea and Brentford footballer. Of course managers were hired and fired, but this was West Ham United – these things didn't happen to us. However success is success and Hammers had gone into freefall down the table after a relegation season. I shouldn't be surprised. It made sense – they had to get someone else while there was still a chance. Before Bobby Moore left.

Bobby Moore? Surely he would have to leave now – he couldn't stay on without Greenwood. Then that really would be it. Everyone knew the story of little Northampton who had climbed up from the Fourth Division to League Division One in 1965-66 – only to drop straight back down again, right back down to Division Four. Could a spectacular fall from grace be round the corner for West Ham United? I had completely forgotten about my trial with Crystal Palace. The future of my football club was now hanging in the balance.

Something would have to be done.

'Speculation' and 'rife' seem to have always been great bedfellows, and the next few days did nothing to keep them apart as far as the Boleyn Ground was concerned. Everyone in a football management position it seemed was to be connected with the West Ham United job, even those in full time managerial employment.

For a mere mortal football follower, understanding just exactly what goes on behind the scenes at any one time in a given season remains several steps behind even knowing about the events. Up until Greenwood's dismissal, the club had an enviably small number of different managers. First up, Syd King ran the shop from 1902 until 1932, to be replaced by Charlie Paynter who took the club through the Second World War to Ted Fenton's appointment in 1950. Ron Greenwood, the fourth manager, was appointed in March 1961, and had run the club over nine successful years until December 1970.

Fenton had departed with West Ham four points clear of the relegation zone by mid-March 1961. After six games without a manager (1 win, 3 draws, 2 defeats) Greenwood was appointed, and his first four games saw three draws and a defeat. Three games into the following (1961-62) season and he was still a winless manager. It was his eighth effort against Spurs – the first ever game under West Ham's new £30,000 floodlights – that Greenwood finally broke his duck. He then won six of the next eight games, his side scoring 21 goals in the process, and Hammers finished eighth.

So what went wrong? Pretty much everything since the summer of 1966 it would seem. I had long dreamed of someone like Jimmy Greaves coming to Upton Park, but not at any point since he had scored those World Cup Final goals had that idea been even worthy of the status of daydream. All that West Ham had in terms of players likely to get them back into the First Division now were, apart from a couple of Greenwood signings, home-grown players. This was the West Ham United (currently managerless) First XI: Bobby Ferguson, John McDowell, Frank Lampard, Billy Bonds, Alan Stephenson, Bobby Moore (captain), Harry Redknapp, Clyde Best, Geoff Hurst, Trevor Brooking and Roger Morgan, with Ronnie Boyce as substitute. With forthcoming games against Hull City, Carlisle and Oxford United – not to mention an FA Cup tie away to First Division Blackpool, the next few weeks were bound to be miserable.

My personal luck, however, always seems to work on a ratio inversely related to the fortunes of West Ham. This was why I suddenly came out from the gloom of the Second Division League Table to start feeling a bit more optimistic about how the weeks ahead might be about to unfold.

Chloe was working in Julian's, a posh hairdresser's down in Swiss Cottage, and getting quite a good wage – not that she needed the money – but she would often cut the hair of the show business set – a clientele that was now beginning to include some of the top First Division footballers. She had already cut Peter Osgood's (League's top goalscorer last year with 31) hair twice – I told her having looked at his latest publicity photos that maybe she shouldn't consider bragging about that one – and then there were visits from John Hollins, Alan Hudson and Arsenal's Peter Marinello.

We had been going steady for nearly six months, though Charlie's thing with Hanna had petered out back in September. This is down to Charlie, though, who is a bit of a character. The footballer's life seems to be made for him, though it doesn't pay as well as you read in some of the papers. I mean I don't think I'd like him going out with my sister – not that he's going to, as she's only two, but you take my point. He has one eye for himself and the other for Charlie. That's who he's looking out for.

We have started going out of a Friday evening to *Orleans*, this night club in Barnet. I now look quite old for my age, and even though it'd take Charlie until 1978 to grow anything he could call a beard, he seems to be able to blag it. It could be that he likes me coming along to take the heat if any questions are asked.

Last Friday, the week after Ron Greenwood got the sack, we both turned up at eleven, having been at the Builders Arms for most of the evening. We'd each told our parents we would be staying over at the other's that night. There was no way my dad would ring to check, and Charlie's dad didn't really care, so that was all sorted.

For a so-called elite nightclub, *Orleans*, from the outside, is a tiny half-varnished mahogany door in an otherwise flush white brick wall with a faint sheen of North Circular Road grime clinging to its surface. Nevertheless, step off the pavement and duck your head into a face full of the speckle stained maroon carpet, and you are soon (after handing over two pound notes) swamped by the warm smoky atmosphere of Henry Cooper after shave and the smell of Watneys.

'You get the drinks,' Charlie said, though the transparency of his comment was partly mollified by the five pound note he was pushing at me.

We were soon sitting in one of the few corners of the room where there was sufficient light to see each other, but not quite enough to work out whose was the lager and whose the bitter.

'Is this the kind of place the Palace players go?' I said, once the gorilla on the door had eased up on giving Charlie the too-young-to-be-in-this-place frown.

'The unmarried ones,' Charlie said. 'Trouble with Palace is they have to go local. It's partly the fact that most of them are pig ugly, partly the fact that no-one would recognise them anywhere north of Wandsworth.'

'How many girls would recognise footballers anyway?' I said. 'Unless you're George Best or Peter Osgood, they wouldn't know.'

'Oh they know,' Charlie said.

The guy on the door had begun to make his way over to our corner with an unpleasant sense of determination.

'What're you having?' I said to him, pushing my way past Charlie and dodging the drinking clientele blocking my path to the bar. I met him halfway but he stood his ground.

'How old's your mate?'

'Don't you know who that is?' I said. We both looked back at Charlie.

Unfortunately the little light there was fell across the soft down of bum fluff on his chin. The power of my words evaporated into the beery swill.

'Nope. Who is it? The Milky Bar Kid?'

I pulled the arm of the doorman gently round before leaning over conspiratorially.

'That's Charlie Barth. Plays for Crystal Palace.' I widened my eyes for effect.

'Under 14s?'

'He's in the Reserves,' I said. 'So come on. What'll you have?' I'd managed to pull him the ten yards needed to get him back to the bar, but he now looked even less convinced than before.

'No kidding,' he said with a smile, after shaking his head. 'I thought I recognised him.' Now it was my turn to gawp.

'You recognised him. How?'

'I'm a regular at Selhurst. Your mate was in the programme last week, in the 'One to Watch' section.' He pointed at the Watneys sign and the barman pulled him a pint without emotion. 'He ain't 18, though, so stay over in that corner or I'll have to chuck the pair of you out.' I left ten bob at the bar and returned to Charlie.

Seated alongside him was a girl in a garish green sequined dress, who seemed to have materialised out of thin air.

'This is Janice,' he said.

'You a Palace fan?' I asked.

'She hates football,' Charlie said.

'I hate football,' she said.

'She's got a mate,' Charlie said. I looked behind me where their eyes were trained, and there was, how can I put it, her mate. Blonde and wearing a dress that looked as though it was stored nightly in an aerosol can. This was Vanessa.

Just how do they end up at clubs like this, girls like that? But that's the kind of person I am, more concerned with the hows and whys than the wherefores. Nevertheless, she provided reasonable company throughout the evening in terms of a way of keeping my balance on the dance floor and somewhere to put my hands other than my pockets.

'You can't go back now,' Charlie said, some time later as we stood outside the club.

'I still play for the First XI on Saturday mornings, Charlie.'

'But what about, you know,' he said, indicating Vanessa with his own subtle version of neck whiplash.

'She's nice,' I said. 'Aren't you?' I smiled at her. It's rude to talk about people in the third person when they're in your presence, or so my English teacher always told me. It was something he had hated about the way his mother had treated him as a child. From the moment I had heard the story I had recognised the genesis.

'Last chance,' Charlie said. He appeared to be using his right hand to examine the brand of knickers Janice might be wearing. Janice smiled, the better part of a bottle of Cinzano dispatched down her gullet over the previous three hours.

'I've booked us a taxi,' I said.

'Well, well. Where are we all going?'

'I'm going home. But you're welcome to have a lift. Where do you all live?'

It turned out the girls were local, and with most of our money sitting in the bar till back inside the club, it was obvious that there would only be finance enough for one taxi. Hardly the kind of situation likely to make me fantastically popular with Charlie, even though he probably owed his tenancy at the bar that evening to the lifelines on my older-looking face. I was still setting him up to score, just as I had done in our earlier days of football together – it was up to him to tuck the chances away.

Ron Greenwood's successor was finally announced on Friday 18th December, the last Friday before Christmas, so we'd have most of the holiday period to mull over it, and so West Ham, supposedly, would have a few games in which to get the squad behind the new boss before the New Year.

I'd wanted Derby County's Brian Clough – the man who had taken his side to fourth place in the First Division in 1969-70 in their first season after promotion, but he wanted to stay to finish the job. Then there was Tony Waddington of Stoke City. An unfashionable Midlands club (in every sense of the word), Stoke had finished the 1969-70 season in 9th position, but he still wouldn't have been my choice. The only other 'outsider' in the frame (Greenwood was the first Hammers manager to be appointed from outside the club) was Bob Stokoe, manager of Carlisle, who elected, somewhat surprisingly, to go to Blackpool – who West Ham would be facing in the FA Cup Third Round in the New Year. They were still in the First Division, but Stokoe had managed Charlton Athletic earlier in the sixties, which should've shown him something about London to endear him to an Upton Park appointment.

In the event, West Ham plumped for 38 year old Noel Cantwell, a major player with the club in the fifties, who had just taken Coventry City from 20th position to 6th place in the First Division in one season – 1969-70. Cantwell had captained and played more than 200 games for the Hammers between 1953 and 1961 before moving to Manchester United for a then record £30,000. He was a versatile footballer, winning 36 caps for the Republic of Ireland, and had proved his managerial pedigree by turning a crock of shite twice-nearly-relegated Sky Blues' Coventry side into a team that had finished four points above his own beloved Manchester United.

Quite why he might have wanted to come down to West Ham was probably in the small print of his contract or down to some nostalgic reverence for the East End and Cassetarri's coffee bar. This was the Barking Road unofficial Hammers' plotting room where he, John Bond, Malcolm Allison and several other great Hammers of the past had spent their weekday afternoons, planning the demise of many a First Division side on their way to playing at the Boleyn Ground that Saturday. In spite of Bobby Moore, it had been Cantwell who had captained the side to a 6th place finish in the 1958-59 season. It had also been Cantwell who had recommended the selection of Bobby Moore to manager Ted Fenton, ironically for a game against Manchester United that the Hammers had won 3-2 to take them in September 1958 to the top of the First Division.

Did I give a shit? There was some other talk in the paper about John Lyall, a 31 year old who last played for the club in May 1963 two seasons after Cantwell left, being appointed manager of the reserves. It seemed a bit of a sympathy job as far as I could see, for a player who had been crocked at 23 and who had never played for the side again. Perhaps the Board had felt it might sway criticism from the sacking of Greenwood, though there was another rumour that it had been Greenwood himself who had sanctioned the appointment.

The good news was that Bobby Moore seemed to be pleased about Cantwell getting the job, from the few quotations I had read. A bit of the new blood / old blood combination could be just what West Ham needed, and this was a man with a recent history of success, too, so I wasn't exactly complaining.

This was more than could be said for Coventry City who were currently fourth in the First Division, and felt they had been robbed of their Championship Manager. There was talk of a contract breaker pay-off, and the bearded chin of Jimmy Hill used all the media nous he possessed to bad mouth the Hammers Board, but the move went ahead. It was an expensive affair for the Hammers, whose Board had often been accused of being stingey – would Cantwell be given any money to buy players? Could he lure any of the top Coventry players (Ernie Hunt? Willie Carr?) to the West Ham United Academy?

Cantwell made a typical Hammers' managerial career start on his first full day in the job with a 3-0 defeat away to Hull City, but my mind for once wasn't on that weekend's game. My trial at Selhurst Park was just over a week away.

Charlie had forgiven my focused decision about the taxi some weeks back, and had been filling me in on everything and anything at the club that might come in handy as a tie-breaker if I was up against a shed load of brainfreak schoolboy footballers. Looking at December 1970 as the potential beginning of a football career for me, I could see that there were many amazing things happening in the world. The North Tower of the World Trade Centre had just been completed, skying out at 1,368 feet, the tallest building in the world. I'd been to the Post Office Tower the previous summer with the school, and felt that was big, but this building was more than twice its size. Even Jack Charlton might need a stepladder to look over the top of it.

On the morning of the 28th December 1970, it seemed as though everything had been frozen. The back garden was like concrete, and it wasn't looking like a great day for a football trial. There hadn't been any games in the League since the 19th December, so it wasn't looking like much would be happening today. Typical British Christmas. All of this had looked at the time to be a ludicrously fortunate opportunity – a combination of nepotism, terrifying good luck and perhaps a nailscrape of talent – and now the British weather might be about to mess it all up. However, as we hadn't heard anything, I decided I would still make the journey to Selhurst Park, even if I had to get there by reindeer.

I got to the ground twenty minutes early, into an area of London that looked even more frozen than Hendon. An abandoned coke bottle lay at the side of the road symmetrically split down the middle, its dark frozen contents forming a bottle-shape emerging from between the glass sections. This was the sort of thing our Art teacher would spend a whole lesson talking about. All it did now was convince me I was about to waste half a day freezing to death in South London.

The locals might have a shit team to support, but at least they got decent TV reception. The giant Crystal Palace transmitter towered up in the distance. So – what to do? I wandered round the side of the ground, past towering locked gates, each one painted with great streaks of frost, icy to the touch.

Charlie had offered to come when I rang him the previous night, but I'd said no. It was enough that he'd set me up for the disappointment – didn't want him to see me suffering it first hand and then feeling he had to tell me how unlucky I was over the next three months. My dad had encouraged me to go, but didn't bring me – the car wouldn't start – he wasn't up to the public transport schlep either, so here I was, alone, on a failed mission.

Life is like that for providing supposed great opportunities, throwing you into the land of the unknown, and then leaving you there. Some road to fame.

Then I heard it – a gate swinging open around the corner. I shot off across the road in the direction of the sound, skidded on a patch of something frozen and went flying into the kerb on the other side of the road.

I looked down at my right hand. The palm was a mess, the wrist cut open with the tear of shingle and stones, and it ached. I stood up. Thank God I wasn't auditioning for the part of Palace Keeper. I wiped the blood on the side of my coat and moved more sedately to the next street.

'You a triallist, son?' the man at the gate said. I looked at him strangely until I realised he was looking at my sports bag.

'Yeah. Is it on today?' The man looked up at the sky, as if he might find the answer there.

'We didn't have the chance to let people know otherwise, so Mr Head asked me to come down and meet up with the lot of you down here.'

'The lot of you' seemed a ridiculous phrase until I looked behind me and saw six other boys my age who had clearly arrived in the last few minutes.

'You cut yourself, son?' I looked down at the blood dripping off my wrist.

'Er, yeah – it's nothing.' I looked where I had been wiping it. A horribly stained coat – that was going to make me popular at home.

I got the wrist bandaged up inside and Mr Challenor, the man at the gate, gave us all some hot drinks and put us in a room to change. I'd already seen the frozen pitch and the tarpaulin cover that a team of horses had dragged across it, so where we might be playing was a bit of a mystery. Palace's game against Chelsea two days earlier had been postponed because of the snow, which was now piled high around the side of the pitch alongside a couple of hired-in tractors and something that looked like a geriatric snow plough.

The true nature of the task ahead of us revealed itself once we had got into the oversized maroon and light blue Palace tracksuits and out onto the pitch.

Ninety minutes of shovelling and dragging later, and the bluey-green surface was clear. There had been much speculation amongst us, during the shovelling, that this might all turn out to be some elaborate trick to get extra help in for pitch clearance, but the sight of John Sewell and Mel Blyth at the side of the pitch as we came off, suggested otherwise.

We brought out two sets of five a side goalposts and were divided into two teams playing widthwise across the pitch. By this time there were ten of us, and Sewell and Blyth took five each and the match was on. By some miracle I had thought ahead enough to bring my plimsolls rather than my boots which meant I kept on my feet throughout most of the game, unlike the other players.

After we'd changed, we were given a hot drink and went up to meet the manager Bert Head who had apparently been watching from the stands. He told us that they had asked twenty boys to come to the ground that day, so the maths doubled the opportunity we had all started with that morning.

I'd played quite well but the surface had been just like concrete, and even with my limited knowledge of the game, I realised that no-one could have told too much from that forty minute kickabout. John Sewell, who was our captain, was very encouraging in everything he said. As I left the ground in the afternoon, I felt I hadn't bolloxed up too badly, which meant that I could take the next three months' worth of condolences without smarting under the caustic sting of irony.

We'd all given our names and addresses to the manager, which was odd as you'd have thought he would have had them from the replies we had sent in over a month back. The sun came out as we left the ground just after two, and things seemed good. I couldn't work out why Tony Taylor hadn't been there, as Charlie had told me that he would be organising the whole trial thing, and was most likely to be taking the session. Now I know what I know, it suggests some rather good things about Crystal Palace from those days, but we were kids then and couldn't have possibly had an inkling of what was really going on, even if some of us did have mates playing in the Reserves.

Dad was surprisingly chatty when he got home that night, but frustrated by my answers about what had gone on at the ground. He seemed to want either to countersign my contract or to offer me the plumbing apprenticeship he'd been going on about in the last week since his best mate's son had signed up for one starting the following April.

This was one of those times when I felt the balance of power over my life shifting from dad to me. There was something strangely pushy about him now he knew I was seventeen; as though my life should now be completely sorted out, my vocation announced and the name of my future wife committed to an expensive sheaf of gold-plated stationery invitations.

The one person I did talk it over with that evening was Charlie. If anyone might have a realistic perspective on the events, it was him.

'I don't know how well I played, but I was okay.'

'I can't think why Sewage showed up – unless it's the manager getting him involved with the youth side of things. Still, that's a good sign, I reckon. Blythy would be there if Sewage was, that's obvious. Do you want me to ask around next week?'

'Not a chance,' I said. 'I'm happy to wait to see what comes through the front door in the next few weeks. I'm in no hurry to drop everything to go and play football.'

It sounded like a putdown, but that wasn't how I'd meant it.

'Palace are a good side, you know,' Charlie said. 'We can get 55,000 in at Selhurst Park – that's nearly 15,000 more than West Ham. And we're in the First Division.'

He was right. And this was when I began to let a bit of air out of the balloon marked 'My Future'. It wasn't good to expect anything after a forty minute kick-about on a bone pitch.

1971 was when things started to change. The unthinkable news that Paul McCartney had split the Beatles on New Year's Eve was only eclipsed by Charlie's revelation about a Palace player and some model called Gemini Reynolds. We all thought it was a bit of a laugh, but everyone had been told to button it in case the story got out to the press.

West Ham's game against Blackpool in the FA Cup ended in a 0-4 debacle, which was further contaminated when it was revealed that Brian Dear, Bobby Moore, Geoff Hurst and Clyde Best had all been out the night before at some Lancashire nightclub, bopping and carrying-on into the small hours. It wouldn't have happened at *Orleans*. Noel Cantwell dropped all four for the next league game, which was a 1-0 victory over Arsenal, the only goal scored by Roger Morgan from a shot that all of us there watching knew he'd meant as a cross.

Maybe the Hammers Board knew something we didn't. Either that, or Noel Cantwell had been a very fortunate appointment. From the reshuffling of the team after the Blackpool cup defeat, Cantwell put a run together of seven successive wins that took Hammers to fourth position in the Second Division table at the beginning of March 1971.

The remarkable thing was that Cantwell had not bought a single player, but had still added something to the team, whether it was motivation, inspiration or the old-fashioned fear of having to play for their places every week, whoever they were. Then there was Geoff Hurst, the forgotten man from 1966, who I still prayed every week would recapture the form that had earned him a place in the England side and who, but for the radius of a football and the whim of a Russian linesman, might have been in that England World Cup winning team. He had returned to the side after the 'Long Weekend' in Blackpool, as it had been termed by the press, and had scored eleven goals in those seven victories, the last three in a magical hat-trick over Sunderland.

While West Ham were returning to form under their new leader, I had earned a second and then a third trial with Crystal Palace. A letter had arrived quite quickly after the frozen bone pitch game, sent to my teacher Mr Greengate at the school, asking him to inform me I was to attend at the Holmesdale training ground in Beckenham at the beginning of February. It was a very different affair to the haphazard nature of the December day, and Tony Taylor was there this time with other players from the team. It was run like a tournament, with twenty of us divided up into four teams, each one playing the other in three ten minute games. Although my side finished runners-up, we played well, and I got an invite back a fortnight later. This was the real moment, a day I'll never forget – the 15th February 1971 – as it was also Decimalisation Day, the day the pounds, shillings and pence became mere pounds and pence.

We had been told that we would all get twenty minutes play during an eleven a side game on the main pitch. It seemed a bit luck of the draw – like performing on the day in an exam, but it didn't bother me. What was a little unnerving, however, was meeting Mr Greengate there, and being told I had made this game from two hundred hopefuls that Palace had been watching over the last six months. He might have told me that after I went on to play my twenty minutes, but once he had, the effect seemed to help. I was given a number six shirt – the number that Bobby Moore was still playing in for the Hammers – and was put in on the left side of midfield. In those twenty minutes I managed to put our number seven through twice, and he scored after the second pass. Added to that I managed a few decent crosses and a shot from outside the area that clipped the bar on its way over. Most of the players that were in my team on that Monday were called back for Tuesday night training, which is what I've been attending ever since. A decision will be made about our future with the club at the end of the season, after we've been there for the next couple of months. We don't get paid, but no-one is complaining about that. Charlie's told me to keep my head down and do my best, and he reckons I'll have half a chance.

Never mind about a game of two halves, what about a season of two halves? With two games to go, West Ham United have climbed to second in the table, just a point behind Arsenal and with a game in hand. The only team that can catch us are Leicester City, who we play tonight at Filbert Street. If they win, they will go level with us. Even if they draw, they could still catch us in the final game, but if we win, we are promoted.

It is West Ham's fantastic away form this season – ten wins out of twenty – that makes me feel optimistic. And that's not to mention how brilliantly Moore, Hurst and Morgan have been playing in all of this. Although I haven't been to many away games this season due to school and Palace commitments, I've decided I have to go. Charlie is playing for the reserves at Plymouth, so he's out of the picture – Chloe is working and my dad is sulking, so I'm going on my own. What else is a fan if he can't go to the matches on his own. You wouldn't be seen dead going to the pictures on your own, you wouldn't go down the pub on your own – unless you were meeting someone there – you wouldn't go out to a club or for a meal on your own. I guess football matches are still one of the few things we can attend alone.

I get there stupidly early at half past twelve, but I haven't got a ticket and I don't want to get locked out. I've heard that there are ten thousand Hammers' fans travelling up, so I'm up there early before the coaches arrive.

The doors open at quarter past one, and I'm in the ground five minutes later, with a programme and a burger with onions – boiled rather than fried it seems. Why do they do that?

The teams are announced at half two, and I make the necessary changes to my programme with my West Ham United lucky biro. Hurst is in – top scoring at the moment with twenty, followed close behind by Clyde Best with eighteen. Both are playing this afternoon.

Leicester City: Shilton, Nish, Whitworth, Cross, Sjoberg, Manley, Glover, Weller, Fern, Sammels, Farrington. Sub: Smith.

West Ham United: Ferguson, McDowell, Lampard, Bonds, Stephenson, Moore (captain), Redknapp, Best, Hurst, Brooking, Morgan. Sub: Lindsay.

Leicester have only lost one match at home this season, to Arsenal back in September, and they don't look like a team who are out there to lose today. You have to go back to Noel Cantwell's first game in charge back in December to see the last time Hammers lost away from home, so it does look like it might be a draw. If Hammers win, though, they are promoted – whatever happens. It's the kind of knowledge that calls for a great performance.

For the first time for a while, I feel supremely confident. Dangerously confident, West Ham fans might say. They've had previous little to cheer about since England won the World Cup five years ago. Relegation last season was the nadir. Today could be the Return of the Academy.

The teams come out, Hammers in their away strip of all light blue with two claret hoops, applauding the thousands of Hammers fans who have made the journey up the M1 and on the train from St Pancras to Filbert Street.

It's a scrappy first half – both sides are clearly nervous, and Leicester have the only real chance with a header from defender David Nish that goes just wide of the post with Ferguson well beaten.

In the second half, Cantwell brings on Jimmy Lindsay for Harry Redknapp, who seems to have had a knock, and the game changes. Lindsay, a slight winger, makes several runs down the right, putting over delicate crosses to the far post, aiming at Clyde Best, but Best is well marked by Sjoberg and Cross, who give him little room. After Jon Sammels has had a shot fingertipped round the post by Ferguson, Hammers make the break that will crown an amazing season.

Bonds and then McDowell take the ball out of defence and Lindsay is given space out on the right to run at Whitworth, but instead of heading out to the wing, he puts a ball into the path of Frank Lampard who has unexpectedly joined the attack, and Lampard hits a swinging, bending, unstoppable shot from fully thirty-five yards past Peter Shilton!

The crowd go stark raving bonkers.

'I'm Forever Blowing Bubbles' starts to resound around the ground as the minutes tick away. Leicester City can't get the ball. Moore is majestic, spraying thirty yard passes around the ground like he's on a training pitch. Bonds is determined, long-legged, a quality player. Brooking is telling with his runs and quality passes. In the end, we've won it at a canter. We are back in the First Division and the fans are singing Noel Cantwell's name! He's soon out with the players for a lap of honour in a ground that the East End fans have taken over. I am singing, hoarse from the effort, roaring, shouting, squeaking, loving the moment.

The following week we beat Luton Town 3-1 at home, and win the title. It's doubly satisfying as we pull away from Arsenal who are beaten on the last day away to Millwall. They are back in the first division with us and have the division's top goalscoring partnership in John Radford and Ray Kennedy. It is a very satisfying final League Division Two Table, and represents the first successful season for me as a fan since I began following the Irons.

		P	W	D	L	F	A	Pts
1	West Ham	42	23	13	6	57	30	59
2	Arsenal	42	21	14	7	73	49	56
3	Leicester C	42	20	13	9	64	41	53
4	Sheffield U	42	20	13	9	65	43	53

Unbelievable. Now all I need to make this season complete is for that letter to arrive on my doorstep from Crystal Palace. So long as the news is good.

CHAPTER FOUR

Debutant

The next year was swollen with events of hysterical unpredictability. Unbeknownst to me, my career in football had begun to crystallise at the Palace. Had the side been riding high in the table during the various trials I had had with the club, things may have been different. As it was, 1970-71 was a problem season at Selhurst Park, a season from which the club was finally relegated from the First Division by a single point.

The people in charge of the youth team seemed to change every week. The three trials I went to before joining were all taken by different players or officials at the club, and when I was finally told that the club wanted me, the signing up process took almost a month, and the day before I was due to sign, the manager Bert Head was sacked.

'It means you're on the club's books,' the dark blue-suited woman in the office stated, after looking at the sheet of paper in her hand for a good couple of minutes. 'It's not an offer of permanent employment, and the club can terminate the agreement at any time. If you make good progress then you may be given a contract at the end of the season.'

'Where's the manager?' my dad said. He was looking at me as he spoke, not at this woman we'd only met in the club's offices five minutes ago.

'Mr Head has left the club by mutual consent,' said the woman, smarmily. 'Yesterday.' She addressed me, directly, as if I was the one who'd asked him to leave. I looked at the agreement she handed me, countersigned as it was by Bert Head. It was as though the words on the page had rearranged themselves spontaneously to read 'Big Ears of Toytown'. And Bert Head had a fair pair of big ears on him, it had to be said.

'It'll be fine,' the woman said, sensing my unease. 'All the agreements were ratified last week.' She addressed the last part of this to the person on the end of the line she had just picked up the phone to. 'Crystal Palace Football Club, Jennifer speaking …'

Dad indicated the door with a swift glance and we were on our way. This was hardly the kind of ceremony I had expected to crown joining my first football club. It was not unlike the particularly unpleasant recurring dream I often had of waking in bed after a night with Chloe to find myself next to Mrs Jennings, our bearded toothless neighbour, who seemed to spend most of her life pottering round her doorstep with the end of a dead cigarette hanging off her lower lip, looking for the postman.

I wasted no time in recounting the events to Charlie that same evening.

'Jennifer Aylott – been at the club for years. Works in the club shop as well as showing the nobs round on match day.'

'Nobs?'

'She was also the old gaffer's secretary, and you can bet she knows the reason why he got the sack. I can't imagine "consent" had anything to do with it. Relegation after just two seasons in the big league, that'll be the reason. The manager picks the team and carries the can.'

'Who was there when you signed your forms, then?'

'Challenor – wearing that car park attendant's coat he's always wearing – though I did meet up with Bert Head the same afternoon. I wouldn't worry – it's not like they'll let us go when we hardly earn anything in the first place. We're probably the safest players on the staff, and the way the place is being run there's a good chance we'll both be in the first team by Christmas.'

It certainly wasn't the glamour profession I had imagined as I rearranged the tabs of my *Shoot!* football league tables that weekend. For all the towering might of the stands on a Saturday at Selhurst Park, it boiled down on a weekday to a woman in a blue suit, a car park attendant and a sacked manager. The matchday might and expanse was an illusion, a temporary edifice against the pounds, shillings and pence – sorry pounds and pence – of a board of directors and badly-paid part-time employees pushing a giant rock up an impossible hill.

Crystal Palace had found there was no way to get back to the top, and the rock had begun to slip back, flattening those that had been pushing it. However, their East London neighbours West Ham United were enjoying the status of 'new boys' for the first time in well over a decade.

I was now in the Upper Sixth at school, having negotiated a path that would allow me to keep my studies going while playing for the Crystal Palace South East Counties Junior 'A' team (or the 'Eagles' as they had been newly nicknamed). There was also the delightful task of following the Hammers under Noel Cantwell as they started their season as well as they had started the previous one badly. Just a quick look at the first ten games in 1971-72 demonstrates the achievements of a newly promoted side.

			F-A
Aug 14 1971	Newcastle (a)	L	0-1
Aug 18 1971	Tottenham (a)	W	1-0
Aug 21 1971	Man Utd (h)	W	3-0
Aug 23 1971	Everton (a)	W	1-0
Aug 28 1971	Derby (h)	L	2-3
Aug 30 1971	Ipswich (a)	D	0-0
Sept 4 1971	Wolves (a)	D	1-1
Sept 11 1971	West Brom (h)	W	4-1
Sept 18 1971	Huddersfield (h)	W	3-0
Sept 25 1971	Nott'm For (h)	W	4-2

Fourteen points from a possible twenty, and Hammers were up to third behind Derby County and Manchester City, both of whom were still unbeaten after two months. Only Derby had beaten West Ham at the Boleyn, though they were so much better on the day that thoughts that the great start might be a mad dream soon returned. Three successive wins at the Boleyn, though, and the fans were right back behind the side as well as they'd ever been.

The problem for me was that suddenly I didn't have the time to get to the games that I had previously enjoyed. Second division football had been less exciting, but I'd seen all of the home games in the relegated season. Now I had sixth form work and three nights and Saturday mornings at Palace, I was only able to get to the Saturday matches, and even then I had to race across London on three different bus routes, at the mercy of London's mercurial public transport system. Luckily all of the West Ham home games had been on Saturday afternoons, but the rest of the season might be a problem.

Watching the game was different now that I was playing for Palace's Under-18s. I'd always played football regularly, always run out for one team or another since I was nine years old, but the perspective had shifted. Others in the crowd went for their vacuum flasks, hot dogs and mugs of Bovril once the half-time whistle was blown. I would watch the expression on the players' faces and try to lip read what they were saying to each other, as they wandered down the tunnel to face the wrath or the smiling face of their manager. It was said that Noel Cantwell was a tough but taciturn man, someone who you'd rather not give a reason to talk to you, if you could help it. He always seemed fairly sanguine to me from my position as a spectator in the West Enclosure.

Dave Spick was our youth team manager. The Northern Irish coach had very little time for anyone who didn't run themselves ragged over ninety minutes for Palace, the kind of demanding attitude that soon had him universally loathed throughout the club. Even the reserves and first team had very little to do with him. Charlie told me they all thought he was a bully.

I got on with anyone and everyone – except my dad – no matter where I found myself. Until Dave Spick. I have no idea what it was about Spick – just who had trapped his nuts in the door as a kid, or held back on the rice krispies portions at the breakfast table – but he hated all the players he coached, and the older you were, the worse it was. As the eldest member of the team, I would get whatever got thrown at us after a defeat. And we did lose most of our matches.

'Nolan,' he'd say. 'On that pitch – *Naaah!*' Some of the players hadn't even finished getting changed, but it didn't matter. After a few games, I only heard the '*Naaah!*' and eventually I found the concentration to imagine that every shout was forcing him closer to the urethral day of reckoning – the arrival of a kidney stone shaped like a golf ball chipped out of jagged flint, that he'd be forced, screaming, to pass into a bucket with all of us watching.

Every tackle I made, every fifty yard run to the corner flag, every jump at the far post, every twist of the neck in the air – they were all driven by the enmity I felt for that man. He never smiled, he never laughed, he just stood there like a plastic sack full of rotting peat, his hair parted barely an inch from his left ear and combed across his head like a night tarpaulin dragged hurriedly over Streatham Ice Rink. And what a man motivator. No wonder we lost all the time. Spick was part of the new regime at Palace that had seen a change in the club crest, and even a change in the nickname from the Glaziers to the Eagles. Birds of prey, it was supposed to symbolise – relegated birds of prey, anyway. The scraps they'd be after wouldn't be anything like as tasty as those available the previous season. But then again, that was the point, I suppose.

Palace had changed drastically since the departure of Bert Head and the arrival of little old me. Arthur Waite had decided, along with vice-chairman Ray Bloye, to appoint the Manchester City coach Malcolm Allison to the manager's post. Allison's success with Joe Mercer at Manchester City and his outspoken nature had made him one of the most talked about personalities in football. Allison was as unlikely a replacement for Bert Head as John Lennon would have been for Russ Conway. He was loud, opinionated, uncompromising and smoked Cuban cigars – even round the training ground. He would think nothing of bad mouthing players who 'weren't up to it' and had more girls waiting for him after training than most of the players. He'd been a player at West Ham during the reign of Noel Cantwell, forced into early retirement after a life-threatening bout of tuberculosis early in West Ham's promotion season of 1957-58. He never got to play in the top flight, and boy was he going to make up for having missed the boat first time round. Worst of all for me, though, he appointed his mate Dave Spick to run Palace's youth team.

We were all supposed to fly the claret and blue flag – the Palace flag, as it was. I kept my version of the flag to myself. A good feature of the relegation of my first ever football club was that my loyalties weren't tested when the first team took to the pitch, though we would be facing West Ham's equivalent youngsters later in the 1971-72 season.

By the time it got round to Christmas, it was clear that Cantwell's West Ham United had enjoyed a honeymoon period that was well and truly over. After the heady start to the season, Hammers hit a slide of form that saw them lose seven of the next ten, and drop within a point of the relegation zone on 19. The thought of going straight down again had perversely drawn me back to events at Upton Park as closely as they could have, after the sense three months earlier that they were getting on fine without my support.

Here was the opportunity for the Board at the club to give Cantwell a few bob to set out a January shopping list to start developing his own side and turn his back on the disappointment of the latter Greenwood years. Whether it was the fear of planning visits to Leyton Orient,

Fulham and other dark places associated with the Second Division, or simply a win on the Premium Bonds, the Board came up trumps, and Cantwell went into the transfer market for the first time to buy the player who had scored the winner against West Ham on the opening day of the 1971-72 season, England international Bryan Robson.

Just how the Geordie was persuaded to leave the acknowledged 'love of his life' wasn't immediately clear, but leave he did, for a club record £200,000. The secret may have been in the figures. One thing I'd learned at Palace was that not everyone was paid exactly the same amount, especially – we'd heard – in League Division One. Could money buy loyalty? The Newcastle fans were furious at their 'spineless money-grabbing' Board – as they saw it – but then Newcastle were only five points above the Hammers, and on a run of form even worse than West Ham's. Hardly the time to sell your top goal scorer, you'd have thought.

I found myself delighted and disappointed at the same time when I heard the news of Robson's arrival. My greatest delight at the Hammers' early form was seeing Geoff Hurst, the forgotten man, beginning to hit the back of the net again. Although four of the six goals he'd scored by the end of October were from the penalty spot, he'd been up there on the goal scoring charts with Clyde Best. Rumours of an alleged problem with alcohol had subsided, and he'd only missed two games. Since November, however, Hurst's goals had dried up again, and the rumours had begun to creep out from under the club floorboards.

Hurst had been photographed several times in a West London bar owned by Peter Osgood and David Webb. It was reported that he had actually been dropped for the fixture at Old Trafford rather than the story about a knee injury that had appeared in the *London Evening News*. When I saw him the following week in a miserable 3-0 home defeat on Boxing Day against Spurs, he looked like he'd aged five years, and put on some serious weight. His cheeks were puffed out this time with fatigue rather than adrenalin.

In the game he 'missed' the week before against Manchester United, Jimmy Greaves had scored two of the goals in a 4-2 Manchester victory. Never had the difference between the fortunes of the two players been so pronounced. But for the call of that linesman back in 1966, the fate of these two men could have been reversed. As it was, Hurst missed the next three games after the defeat against Spurs, and the day after he returned to the side in a 0-0 frozen pitch of a game against

Cantwell's old side Coventry City, the signing of Bryan Robson was announced.

But Hurst had still never struck me as a drinker.

What do I know about drink? – but if it's a choice – to become an alcoholic – then maybe the linesman made that choice for him.

Hurst was involved in that Blackpool furore just over a year ago – what can they do – people who make it to the top – when there is nothing else to achieve? The timing was almost perfect for Hurst, almost. Perhaps that was what made it even worse, to know how close you were to becoming that celebrated, that revered … Football can offer celebrity status to anyone who's good at it. There's the fine line of a little luck, words not said, choices not taken … To what extent does talent really come into it? Maybe the ratio of talent to luck is underestimated.

Bobby Moore continued to play for England throughout West Ham's promotion season back in Division Two – it was the only season of his life where he had played outside of the top league in his country.

He got his 91st England cap against Greece in the European Championship qualifiers last month – only Bobby Charlton (106) and Billy Wright (105) have more than that, and though Jimmy Greaves has 83, he's said it's unlikely he'll play for England again now he's 31 (even though he's still knocking them in for Manchester United).

Of course I still feel as much a Geoff Hurst supporter as I am a West Ham fan. How couldn't I feel that way? If it wasn't for him, I guess none of this would be happening. Bound to him by the mysterious strands of fate that have grown taut across his career, slackening for a year or two before – it seems to me – they will tighten around him again. He doesn't get mentioned much outside of Upton Park these days, as you might expect. Just eight appearances for England, and those three goals, all in 1966 – v Scotland in the 4-3 win in April, the World Cup Quarter-Final winner against Argentina and that header in the World Cup Final. And now, the prospect of football oblivion with the arrival of Bryan Robson who's already scored twice for England in his four appearances. For some, Hurst's achievements would represent glorious high quality moments in a full career, but not me. I know from days that date back to my dream as a twelve year old kid that he could have been so much more.

Chloe has been modelling for her aunt. Why it should piss me off, I have no idea, but it does. She says there's nothing to it, but I've seen the pictures. If those blokes are spending the whole day looking at her cute little bum, well they're bound to try to chat her up too. Who could blame them? It's not as though she's wearing a ring or anything. Like that would make any difference.

Funny thing is, we seem to still be getting it off together. And I have given her no idea that I might be – I don't really want to say the word unless I let the idea out of the bag – jealous or anything. Time was just a year ago that we'd see each other maybe three or four times a week. Trouble is now that I see her Saturday night and maybe once on a Tuesday or Thursday … It does seem to be enough, though. Actually, if you average it all out, we probably do it as much as we did last year. Not exactly going into too much detail, but – you do different things, don't you … once you get to know someone better. Not even as if you need to ask, is it? You just kind of … do it, and there you are. Trouble is that to keep up the average we don't always have the most ideal conditions. She doesn't care, though. I actually think she likes it more when we're, you know, outdoors. 'Al fresco' as she calls it. So I suppose that might be why I worry about her going on all those photography shoots – out to all those different locations. Stretch of the imagination, mine or hers, and then … well, there you are. Or there she is. And there I'm not. If you see what I mean. So I suppose that's why I feel the way I do about her going off getting photographed. It's not exactly smart getting jealous, so I suppose I'll just have to live with it.

Malcolm Allison is getting right up Charlie's nose at the moment. Although Charlie and I are both the same age, he might as well be five years older than me. He's twice travelled up in the first team coach with the squad. First game was at Leicester (Palace's strongest promotion rivals) in November, the ground where I saw West Ham get promotion last season! Then he went up last month to Hull City. He wasn't named sub on either occasion, but we all know it's only a matter of time. So why should he hate the manager when he's likely to give him his first team debut any minute now?

It's nothing at all to do with football. The trouble is that Charlie has taken a fancy to this girl Suzy, who works in the main office. He has been chatting her up, week on, week off – and she seems to quite like him. I've seen her talk to him, and I was one of the ones encouraging him – not that he normally needs any encouragement. However, he finally plucked up the (double whisky) double Dutch courage to ask her out, and she started shaking her head as he's asked her, making signs for him to stop without actually saying it. Before she can explain, the manager is in the room calling him over for a chat about tactics. Looking back at her, he has realised what it's about. So I suppose that's as far as it'll be going.

'But I fancy her, Roy. I've spent the last month tiptoeing round asking her out – that's like you taking a year. I can't believe it. I mean, he's forty-bloody-four, and she's seventeen. It's criminal, Roy.'

'He's the boss, Charlie. And you're this close (gesture with index finger and thumb, not to be confused with how sexually stimulated the thought of her and the boss in action might make us both feel) to getting into the first team. He's practically made you sub twice. You've got to realise, if you don't mind me saying, that you aren't going to have a puff on any cigar that belongs to him.'

'He's an arsehole.'

'He's the boss. Why don't you just go on being nice to her – he might get bored with her in the end, and … She might feel you're worth something for waiting.'

'That's not how it works out. I'm the guy who came second. Once they see you as the also ran, that's what you'll always be. You don't get the chance to come in all fresh for a second go. So maybe you understand why I'm pissed off with him. And that crazy coat he wears. What century does he think he's from? How are we ever going to get promotion if his eyes are in his balls?'

The manager, you should understand, is a man I have yet to speak to. He did acknowledge me once in the corridor at the ground when I came up to watch Charlie in the reserves, but that's it. He probably doesn't even know my name. He's hardly going to be taking an interest in the Junior 'A' team until we start winning. If he's still there when that finally happens.

Charlie is right about the manager's dress sense, though. It is a bit on the outrageous side. And none of it seems to have anything to do with anything that's going on in the real world. He doesn't seem to want to look like John Shaft, Tom Jones or even Marc Bolan – at least I hope he doesn't, because if he's ended up looking like anyone then it's probably Benny Hill.

I realise that I've kind of made it my current mission in life to make sure Charlie avoids messing up his career at Crystal Palace because he is jealous of the power of the manager. Quite how I'm going to do that without messing up our friendship into the bargain is something that might take some working out. Maybe I need to talk to Suzy myself, first chance I get.

Bryan 'Pop' Robson, as he's called, though no-one seems to know why, has already been a veritable machete in the side of the Hammers this season, scoring the winner at St James' Park back in August, and the two goals that saw Newcastle complete the double over the Hammers in December. That was clearly enough for Noel Cantwell, who signed him for £200,000 as the print was still drying on his New Year Upton Park shopping budget cash list.

Hammers could now boast a forward line with two England international strikers, and the Bermudan wonder boy Clyde Best, way ahead of the rest with thirteen goals, and 'Pop' Robson soon got among the goals to drag the Hammers back into the top half of the table after just a handful of matches. Things weren't going too well with Geoff Hurst, however, and some cruel photographs taken by the emerging 'talents' of Fleet Street's finest, accounted for why he wasn't appearing regularly in a West Ham United shirt.

That might have been all I would have ever known about the last season of my hero's dwindling career, but for a turn of fate on a cold February night at Upton Park. I hadn't actually been to see the Hammers play for almost a month, seeing as Dave Spick had finally got us on a winning streak – not, sadly, in the South East Counties league, which we were still propping up like a Clapham Junction railway sleeper – but in the FA Youth Cup. We'd knocked out Cambridge in November, Friern Barnet in December and Orient away in January after drawing at home before Christmas. Then we'd faced Birmingham City in the Fourth Round and beaten them at St Andrews, to earn a plumb tie against West Ham United.

It wasn't just the thought of playing in a game involving my beloved Hammers for the first time in my life, but the reflection that – as with all FA Youth Cup ties in the latter stages – we would be playing at the club's First Team ground, and therefore at the home of the academy of Football, Upton Bloody Park.

West Ham's under-18s were mid-table in the sixteen team league, but had caned us hollow when we'd met them in November. I hadn't played in that particular 4-0 drub-a-dub-dubbing, but I had played in all of the FA Youth Cup games, and was told on the Saturday that I would be in the team against West Ham. For all his boorish mannerisms, I had begun to accept that, despite all his failings, Spick did actually have some kind of an inspirational effect on the team when it came to our cup ties that season. That and the fact that he had unaccountably persuaded Allison to let us play Charlie after bottom-of-the-table Orient had almost succeeding in knocking us out in the home tie.

Having Charlie in the team was about as good as it could get for me as a player that season. Despite our similar ages, Charlie and I had only ever appeared in the same school team up to the age of 13, when Charlie's talent had been noticed by the First XI coach, and he had found himself fast-tracked into the First XI team, playing alongside 17 and 18 year old prefects who'd been giving him detentions just the week before.

Charlie went straight into the Palace youth team at centre-forward, replacing Don Edwards, Mr Bang Bang as we called him, even though he hadn't scored all season.

I was enjoying my best run in the side – five successive matches – playing left midfield in the number ten shirt. It hadn't been a particularly demanding role in the league – just mopping up when our moves broke down and keeping possession. The cup run changed all that. I don't think I have run so far and worked so hard in any side. Our left winger was Gary Bascombe, a speedy forward with skill and pace who could always be relied upon to link up well with me to set up chances for Charlie. Even though he'd only played in the Orient replay and the Birmingham game, Charlie already had four goals, two in each game.

You sensed that the other players somehow raised their game when Charlie played – after all, he was achieving what the others in the side all wanted – standing on the edge of a first team place. We just prayed that Allison would let Spick have him for the cup games till the end of the season. It was quite an ask with a competition that had always had a two-legged semi-final and final. Palace had never had much success in the FA Youth Cup, but we were only three games away from the final, an achievement in itself that would put us in the Palace history books. And winning it? What a farce that would be!

I had little hope, as I saw it, of making the spectacular kind of progress that Charlie had made, even if I was given another three years, but I knew how to make the most of what was around now. A trip to Upton Park, to run out on the pitch, albeit in this crazy Palace strip of one claret and one light blue stripe down the middle of the shirt – another great idea from those trying to turn Palace into the greatest team in London. Impossible to understand just why the Big Board Boys in charge of the club could only generate a sense of ambition after the club had been relegated.

The moment I saw the Big Boss standing by the coach door, puffing on one of his Cuban classics, I knew this was a game the whole of the club was taking really seriously. The first team hadn't played West Ham since the 1969-70 season, but the London rivalry and the chance to go into battle with the side that had produced the two England World Cup Winners Bobby Moore and Martin Peters – maybe Allison fancied his chances of rubbing shoulders with some First Division talent in order that a little portion might rub off on him. Palace still looked a reasonable bet for promotion so far – pity that the boss had to use an FA Cup Youth game to get himself closer to those he wanted to emulate.

Charlie and I had come on the bus from Clapham Common after the train down from Hendon, and now we faced a coach ride across London. We had the first team coach tonight, with its properly upholstered seats and tables for games of cards to keep the first team busy on boring motorway journeys to places like Carlisle and Middlesbrough. Not that we had any cards. Half the players in the team were still reading comics.

This was a real opportunity for me to impress the manager, though there was always the chance that he might be too busy looking around his old club to concentrate on the football out on the pitch. My concern had shifted, though, as I realised my work might be cut out keeping Charlie from saying something stupid over the course of the journey there and the journey back. Spick had been laying into us at training on the Monday night how we had to be 'professional' and how we must make sure we 'give a good account of ourselves'. He didn't want us to show him up in front of Allison – I realised that now. Charlie hated both of them, and didn't really care who knew. I had spoken to Suzy for the first time the previous week, and had the kind of information that could ruin the evening before it had even started.

'You're Charlie's mate, aren't you?'

'One of his fans, really.'

'You went to the same school,' he said. 'Good that, you getting in the team together.'

'I'm nowhere near as good as Charlie. He's the one who's going to make it. Everyone knows that.' It had been easy to talk to her, but now I was there, I suddenly had no idea just how I might broach the subject of her and Allison. I'd planned approaches before, even thought of clever lines into the subject, but they all vanished as I looked at her. She was staring hard at the half-written letter on her typewriter, arms folded.

'What you writing?' I said, finally. 'If it's not confidential.'

'No,' she said, and she laughed. 'Just ordering another suit from this tailor in Savile Row for Mr Allison. He likes the lapels slightly wider than normal, and this bloke makes them how he likes them.'

'Is that what you do?' I said.

'I'm not his personal secretary,' she said, suddenly. 'He just gives me a list of things to get done in the day when I get a spare moment.' She smiled and made a little grimace that could have meant anything.

'Do you like him?' I said, before I'd thought through how the question might sound. It sounded shit.

'He's the boss, ain't he?' she said. 'Everyone likes Mr Allison.'

'Not all the players do,' I said. I was surprised to find that I was surprised to hear her say 'ain't'.

'Oh really? Who in particular?' She was suddenly animated. 'Not Charlie?'

'Why?' I said. I was getting the feeling that I should go before the unsaid got said.

'Just something he said once. I'm always telling him not to have this complex, like my mum says. Everyone has to have a boss. Better to get on with them than to want to get one over on them. Malcolm can do a lot for Charlie.'

'Malcolm?'

'Mr Allison, I mean. He thinks Charlie is good enough to get to the very top.'

'He told you that?'

'He talks to me about the team. At lunchtime, sometimes,' she added.

This was the point where I needed to take the conversation by the scruff of the neck or look for the Way Out.

'I'll see you then,' I said. It sounded horribly shallow, but I didn't want to know what she knew and what she would almost certainly let me know by her reaction if I asked her.

Charlie and I sat at the back of the coach. It was a 7.30 pm kick-off so leaving at 5.00 might have been seen as cutting it a bit fine. Then again, this was the Young Eagles, a team who had only won five matches all season, and four of them in the cup.

67

The weird thing was that I had still yet to play on the hallowed Selhurst Park turf (unless you counted the frozen kick-about last season at my post-Christmas 'trial'), but here I was this evening, about to run out onto the Boleyn Ground, where Bonds, Brooking, Hurst and Moore regularly strolled out of a Saturday afternoon. What would it feel like? Glory!

'What did she say, cloth ears?' Charlie shouted. I was miles away.

'Big boss came in just as I was about to pop the question.'

'What an arsehole.'

'He didn't do it deliberately – just bad timing, really.'

'No such thing as bad timing with that prat. If it happens and he's in the room, it's down to him.'

'The buck stops with the manager,' I said.

'If only his bucks had stopped. It wouldn't surprise me if …'

'You two planning the downfall of the mighty Hammers?'

Charlie's feeble nostrils had not twitched to the aroma of the Cuban Cutlass. We were no doubt about to suffer a Malcolm Allison pep talk. I could see Spick's concerned face at the front of the coach looking down the aisle, in frozen fear of a misjudged utterance from his two seniors.

'When did you last play at Upton Park?' I said hurriedly, keen to black out anything Charlie might say now and think about later.

'September 9th 1957. Sheffield United. We got beat 3-0. First home defeat of the season. We lost the next two as well. 3-2 at Swansea and 2-1 at Sheffield United. That was when I knew something was wrong.'

'You should have realised after a 3-0 home defeat, boss,' Charlie said.

'That would have had me worried.'

Charlie wore the trace of a smile that made it clear just what he had meant by the comment.

'I had tuberculosis you little twat,' Allison snapped. 'My playing career was finished eleven days after my thirtieth birthday. I nearly died. How old are you – eighteen?'

'Next month,' Charlie said. He didn't look in the slightest bit worried.

I'm supposed to stop this kind of thing happening, I was thinking. How did I get us here?

'Just make sure we're in the semi-finals tonight, Barth,' Allison said, drily. 'If you want to play for the Juniors again.' He was back in his seat at the front of the coach before I could even process the words. Spick threw the two of us a heavy glare, even though it was unlikely he'd heard what had been said. I couldn't reassure myself. Allison's tone had been unambiguous.

'So there you go,' Charlie said. 'All the fun of the fair.'

'Well done, Charlie. Threw your career away for a funny line.'

'Yeah.'

'And it wasn't even funny.'

'Fuck him,' Charlie said. 'And his fucking teenage harem.'

I sank back into the chair. It suddenly felt that I was sitting on a tablet of stone. My backside ached like I'd taken one almighty kick from an unscrupulous defender on my way over the advertising hoardings into touch. This game I was now just over an hour away from should have been the sporting moment of a lifetime – running out at the ground I must have visited over a hundred times as a fan – but all I could think about was how I was going to patch things up between the Big Boss and Charlie. It seemed to me that if I let Charlie mess things up for himself at Crystal Palace, then it would be the end of my career, too. We'd been told that there were likely to be up to 5,000 at Upton Park, all screaming the Hammers on to their place in the semi-final draw.

Pissballs.

CHAPTER FIVE

Common Market

Dave Spick had taken his youth team into the quarter-finals of the FA Youth Cup in January 1972, the best achievement of any Crystal Palace Youth team since they'd had one. Edward Heath had taken the country into the Common Market, or the EEC (European Economic Community) as it was known, in the same month, a feat equal in historical stature, you might say. In a similar parallel, underpinning these two epic achievements, there were now one million unemployed people in the United Kingdom and a national state of emergency, declared in the light of the miners' strike. On the Palace Youth Team front, we'd won just one game in the league, our top striker Charlie Barth had just had a row with the club manager, and was looking at an extended future cleaning other players' boots if he didn't put in a miracle performance over the next hour and a half.

We got off the coach in Green Street, in front of the giant claret iron gates of Upton Park, the doorway to the 'theatre of nightmares' as one journalist had called it after the 1969-70 relegation season.

Eighteen months later, and Hammers were back in the big time. Of sorts. Earlier that week the club had struggled to overcome Southern League side Hereford United in the FA Cup Fourth Round replay, after a nervous goalless draw at Edgar Street. Hereford had already beaten first division Newcastle United 2-1 after a 2-2 draw. This had been on television and had featured some bloke tonking an unstoppable strike from about forty yards. Hammers finally put them out of the cup 2-1, but only after being behind in the match for almost an hour. I'd missed the game as I'd been training in Beckenham, preparing for tonight. And here we were.

The game wasn't having the same effect on the other 'Young Eagles' in the Palace team. You could see it as we got off the coach. Most of them had been more impressed with playing at St Andrews, and still regarded Palace as a team only temporarily outside of the top league. They weren't bothered that West Ham had won the FA Cup and the European Cup Winners Cup, that they had spent twenty-one seasons in the first division to Palace's two.

West Ham's youth team equivalent of Charlie was a young Nigerian striker called Ade Coker, a player who'd already made his debut for the first team, and had even scored on the occasion in a 4-2 defeat at Manchester United. He'd got eleven goals for the youth team, and he would be one of many problems for our leaky defence to contain.

Charlie had captained us in the two cup wins he'd played in but, predictably, Allison decided to hand over the captaincy to Martin Beason before the game. There was nothing wrong with Beason. He'd been youth team captain for most of the season, but the gesture made it clear that Charlie and the Cuban Castigator were no longer an item.

'The manager's told me you're on a tenner each if you can pull it off tonight,' Dave Spick said, his face manic, his eyes glazed. I could smell the familiar trace of alcohol camouflaged under his cigarette breath as he bellowed at us. 'I don't know what your problem is, Barth, but fecking can it for the next ninety minutes. If we can hit this lot with an early goal, they fold. Southampton's kids beat them 3-0 last week. Beason, stop the black kid. Anyway you have to. He's the main danger. Just don't get yourself sent off. Go on then, all of you ... On that pitch ... Naaah!' ... We turned out of the carbolic-soaked concrete rooms in our away strip of white shirts and light blue shorts, our studs clickety-clacking down the tunnel, a single right turn and there they were, to our left, the opposition. Each of their players seemed to have the best part of a foot in height on us, and the keeper was over six feet tall, and grinning like a lunatic.

'Right, Charlie?' said one of the claret and blue shirted players. Charlie turned round.

'Do I know you?' he said.

'No. But you will.'

Whatever Charlie replied was lost in the defeaning cheer from the crowd as we ran out under the bright Upton Park floodlights. I sprinted a good hundred yards across the pitch, an adrenaline pulse taking hold of me as I reached the chicken run over on the East Stand side. If we kicked off towards the South Bank, this would be the strip of turf

I'd be patrolling for most of the first half.

The pitch was soft and would cut up very quickly. The goalmouths both looked like patches of quicksand. This was predictable after the game that had been played here not 48 hours previously. Would I ever play a competitive game in the FA Cup?

'Roy!' I heard behind me. Charlie knocked a ball to me, and I volleyed it back. 'That bloke in the tunnel – Tony Marchant. The mouthy git. He captained Essex schoolboys against Surrey last year, and we had a set-to in the car park.'

'Not like you, Charlie,' I said.

'Well, keep an eye on him. He plays right back, so he'll probably be marking you. Hasn't got much talent, but he'll get stuck in. He's vicious.'

I laughed. So I was playing at the Academy of Football? Why should it be any different from playing at Holmesdale? You usually got threats every other game. If you took them seriously you might as well give up. I was more bothered about protecting Charlie than anything else. Marchant could take his threats and stuff them up his arse.

It was the most prestigious game I had ever played in, and the clubs had made every effort to raise the status of the fixture for the young players like us that night. At St Andrews there had been nearly a thousand fans in attendance, but there looked to be ten times that tonight. Maybe the game had got some added publicity at West Ham's Monday night cup tie, but whatever the reason, we needed no motivation to work at producing the performance of our lives that night.

We started promisingly, and our left winger Gary Bascombe twice got past the defence to hit in a couple of great crosses, but on both occasions Charlie wasn't up with the play and the chances went begging. Spick wouldn't let me wear my watch on the pitch, so I had no way of knowing how much time had elapsed. Despite this, my match time compass kicked in and seemed to indicate close on half time when the first major incident in the match occurred.

One of our many attacks had broken down and I'd been caught in possession, but as they took up the play, a diving tackle by Beason found Charlie loose on the halfway line with only Marchant back to cover him. Charlie picked up some pace from nowhere and began haring down on goal with Marchant chasing. As Charlie rounded the keeper, Marchant threw himself to his right and blocked a certain goal with his hand. It had to be a penalty.

It seems hard to believe, but we hadn't been awarded a penalty all season. Even if we had, the way we'd been playing we would probably have missed it. Now we had as good a chance as any of taking a first half lead and closing down the tie. But who would take it? Spick had made Don Edwards the penalty taker earlier in the season, but Charlie had replaced him, so it seemed logical to assume that Charlie would be the one to take it. However, Charlie had been taking penalties for the reserves since Christmas, and had missed one at Fulham on Saturday in a 0-0 draw.

I looked over at the dugout and although Spick was sat, motionless in his seat, Allison was up in the air, yelling and gesticulating. Beason ran over to get the message as Charlie was putting the ball on the spot. Here we go, I was thinking. Allison doesn't want Charlie to take it.

Beason took his orders and sprinted over to Charlie, but Charlie waved him away dismissively before Allison's words could be delivered. With a three pace run up, Charlie slotted the ball to the keeper's left, and although he got his fingertips to it, the power took the ball home into the corner of the net.

The goal was met by a stony silence from the partisan crowd of kids up at the North Bank end that we were kicking towards, and Charlie ran back to the centre circle without a celebration, pursued half-heartedly by Beason. I managed to get to him before he reached Charlie.

'Just leave it, Beason.'

'But the gaffer said I should take it.'

'He's not the gaffer. Spick is. Did Spick tell you to take it?'

'He is the gaffer of the club.'

'Leave it, Beason,' I said. 'I'll sort it at half-time. Just keep the defence together, for Christ's sake.' Unbelievable. Beason was actually crying, though he was trying desperately to keep the tears back. Fucking Charlie. Why couldn't he just let Allison be a prat and leave it at that?

I realised I was out of position at the sound of the whistle, and ran across the pitch towards the left, but as I looked up I saw that Charlie was somehow through again, on his own, and was tucking the ball in the back of the net for his second goal of the night. I couldn't have taken my eye off the play for more than ten seconds, but that was all that Charlie had needed. This time he was celebrating with Gary Bascombe who, I later discovered, had started the move by intercepting a lazy pass from the kick-off. We were 2-0 up at Upton Park against the mighty Hammers and it wasn't even half-time yet. Fuck!

'And Michael Reece? Three times in the first half I'm watching you wandering around in the midfield. When the move breaks down you have to get back and stay with one of their midfielders. Who were you marking?'

'Their number eleven,' Reece said.

'Well fucking mark him then! Couple of lucky goals and you're playing as if you want to lose the game. Never lose sight of the fact that you're two minutes away from defeat – two minutes! Take control of the game, boys. Take control!'

Allison marched out of the changing-room, puffing at his cigar.

We all looked at each other in bemusement. Even Dave Spick, who'd entered the room halfway through Allison's tirade, had nothing to add to the rant we'd all just witnessed.

'Correct me if I'm wrong,' said a voice at the door. 'But aren't we two goals ahead in this game?' I looked up. It was Charlie. Allison hadn't noticed that he wasn't in the room during his voices-off. Spick got up, gave Charlie a look that would have reduced anyone else to tears, and left.

'I thought you were gonna sort it out, Nolan,' said Beason.

'Fuck off,' I said.

The second half started much more slowly than the first had. We had a lot of possession and knocked the ball around well. West Ham were desperate to get into the game, but couldn't get the ball. Charlie came back to give support to the midfield so that we began to control the game like we hadn't done before. At one stage in the second half, I looked over at the dugout and could only see Dave Spick and Don Edwards, who was sub, both of them sitting there mute, like Southampton away supporters watching their team getting thrashed at Newcastle.

Eventually, you could sense that West Ham had given up. Not only had we kept possession better than them, but we still had something in the tank. The Hammers youth team were spent, drained, defeated.

Looking up high into the directors' box, I could see Malcolm Allison in his giant orange burberry coat, clapping in excitement at his side's victory. He hadn't stayed long in the dugout. Would Charlie's goals help appease their relationship?

Beason pushed the ball to me, and I began to weave my way up the left wing, waiting for Bascombe to come across from the centre, which he did, and I found him with a short pass. Taking the return, I caught Marchant on the wrong foot, and broke away down the left.

'Go on, son!' I heard an old guy shout from the chicken run. It was all the encouragement I needed, as I headed for goal. I had never scored for Palace, despite many chances in the twenty odd games I'd played, but maybe this was it. As I closed in on their giant of a keeper, I saw Marchant chasing back out of the corner of my eye, and across beyond the keeper, waiting, was Charlie. This was the hat-trick – I knew it. As the keeper came out, I steered the ball square to him.

The stadium hushed.

Charlie's face lit up as the ball ran perfectly into his path, onto his right foot, and he hit the shot sweetly, crisply. Somehow, the keeper threw himself backwards and thrust out a hand to tip the ball against the crossbar and over. It was the most fantastic save I had ever seen. Even Charlie patted him on the back as we went up for the corner. Marchant came up behind me and whispered, 'That's the best keeper in the country, mate. Remember his name – Mervyn Day. He'll be in the first team one day.'

The whistle went. There wasn't time to take the corner. A parade of staged handshakes and we were soon heading off the pitch. Music started belching out of the speakers, and the crowd began to disperse.

Spick was waiting at the touchline to greet us. It was the first time I'd ever seen him smile, and from the difficulty he was having, it looked like it was something he didn't do that often. Three of the first team, Mel Blyth, Tony Taylor and Bobby Tambling were also there, clapping us off. What an honour. It would have been even better if Allison had been standing behind them. I knew I now had the courage to tell him how important Charlie was to the team, how it wasn't his fault that he got moody now and again, that he had done what Allison had asked and scored the goals that had got us to the semi-final …

The steam in the changing room when we walked back in could mean only one thing – a proper giant bath. It was big enough to swim in, but all I did was jump in and sit there, luxuriating in the heat and the smell of cheap soap. I hadn't even taken my shirt off.

West Ham had organised some food in an upstairs room for the team, which we ate with their youth team players. They were clearly distraught after missing out on a semi-final place, and didn't have much to say. I looked across at Ade Coker, the Nigerian, who had hardly touched the ball the whole game. He would have more first team success later in the season, though. Another player from that night who would make the first team later on was a tall blond West Ham defender called Kevin Lock.

After we'd eaten, a few celebrities from West Ham who were there to watch the game came in to congratulate us on the performance.

Noel Cantwell was there, whose hand I shook, as well as Alan Stephenson, the centre-half who'd also played for Crystal Palace earlier in his career, with Trevor Brooking and Jimmy Lindsay, who I remember being incredibly shy. I was surprised to find that I had little to say to the players, despite a lifetime of following the team. I have always felt that footballers talk more eloquently with their feet.

Then the unexpected face, a man I had always wanted to meet, behind all of the rest so that I almost missed him as I was about to leave the room, on my way back to the coach. No-one from our team had noticed him, and apart from a few words with Trevor Brooking, he had remained unnoticed even by his own teammates. He sat by the door with a small glass of lemonade and I caught his eye.

'Well done, son,' he said. 'You were the left midfield?'

'Yeah,' I replied. My voice sounded like a twelve year old's.

'That's where I used to play at West Ham before Ron Greenwood put me up front.'

Geoff Hurst. I couldn't believe that he had even recognised me from the game.

I hadn't really thought about my own performance, but in retrospect, it was probably my best game ever for Crystal Palace.

'It was because of you that I took up football seriously,' I said, after about ten seconds of embarrassed silence. It sounded like the most feeble utterance ever, but I knew it was true.

He looked at me with an expression of puzzlement.

'Why was that?'

I was going to tell him about my dream about his Wembley hat-trick, about my dad, who had never believed it was possible, and who wasn't here tonight – tonight – the most important night of my footballing life. About how he shouldn't let things in his career get him down, about how I thought on his day he was still one of the best strikers in the Football League. About how he had been the single most important inspiration in my career; about how I would never have gone into football had it not been for what had happened to him in that World Cup Final.

Maybe it would have made a difference – maybe it might have inspired him in return to hear my story. Whatever the possibilities, the moment was more inspirational for the sudden massive stadium power cut. All the lights went out and we were plunged into profound darkness. After some embarrassed laughter and cries of 'Stop that, Jimmy!' from a female voice or two, a torch was lit, and the evening ended. We were eventually directed down the stairs to the coach by two of the Palace officials who had made the journey with us to the ground. I smiled when I saw that the first of these was Challenor from my trial day last season. I hadn't seen him at the club for ages.

That remains my happiest memory from that early period at Crystal Palace. There weren't many other nights to rival it.

We drew Aston Villa (the eventual winners) in the semi-finals and were beaten 2-0 at Villa Park after the goalless first leg home tie, my first-ever game at Selhurst Park, in front of 10,000 fans. Charlie wasn't allowed to play for us again after the West Ham victory, but not because of his bust-up with Allison. The Cuban Cormorant actually gave him his first team debut the following Saturday against Cardiff City at Selhurst Park, when he came on for the last ten minutes to replace Willie Wallace. He did well in that game, and was in the first team squad for the rest of the season. Suzy left Palace a few days after our quarter-final victory over the Hammers. We never found out why, but for Charlie it seemed to patch things up with the manager. I wondered if he knew. There was a rumour going round that he'd sacked her and I couldn't find anyone sufficiently in the know to scotch it.

I finished my A'Levels and my first year at Palace around the same time. I passed all three – English, French and History, and had continued to keep open the possibility of taking up a place at University. In the end my grades weren't quite good enough to get me to Leeds, which was my first choice, so I decided to defer for a year and see how things went with Palace. They had chosen to keep me on for one more year on a temporary contract, for which I would be paid, but once they realised that the club wouldn't get promotion (they missed out on the 'bounce back' by just three points) then they were into saving every penny they could. It had to be Malcolm Allison's tailor's bill.

Domestically, England's was still arguably the best league in the new 'EEC' and had looked confident and positive in the early stages of the 1972 European Championship, which they were favourites to win. Drawn against Hungary, however, in the two-legged Quarter-Finals without Jimmy Greaves, they lacked any firepower, losing 2-0 in Budapest, and they were only able to muster a hard-fought 1-0 victory at Wembley in the return, the only goal an own goal in the first half by Kocsis. Another strange barren year of international achievement, six years after the World Cup final win. It felt like that 1966 game must have been played in another century, when we had a decent international team, or was it just that everyone else was finally catching up?

West Ham, in their first season back, finished in a very respectable twelfth position under Noel Cantwell, but had laid promising foundations for a quality season thanks to the purchase of Bryan Robson, who had scored fourteen goals, and Clyde Best who had matured into a powerful and determined striker with a magnificent top-scoring season's achievement of 23 – nearly half of our total for 1971-72.

	P	W	D	L	F	A	Pts
11 Wolves	42	15	11	16	49	52	41
12 West Ham	42	13	13	16	56	48	39
13 Stoke	42	11	16	15	39	53	38
14 Ipswich	42	12	12	18	47	63	36

It's hard to look at those statistics now with any scientific analysis. Was there any hidden warning that this mid-table performance might suggest what would happen in 1972-73?

Just what is it that makes any one team better than the team the year before? It can sometimes be the same players and a different manager, or one new player whose arrival transforms the whole side and gets all of them playing to a level that none of them realised they could play to before.

The sides who were setting the standards at this time were Don Revie's Leeds United, Brian Clough's Derby County and Bill Shankly's Liverpool. Teams from the Midlands, Lancashire and Yorkshire. There was no-one from London to fly the flag. Not since Tottenham's 'double' of 1960-61 had anyone from the capital shown Championship potential. Arsenal, under Bertie Mee, had finished eighth in their first season back, but with only nine more points than West Ham.

Nevertheless, Noel Cantwell bought well in the close season, securing the services of Bill Garner from Southend, a lanky forward who was brought in to fill West Ham's third striking position, left vacant since the departure of Geoff Hurst. Cantwell also bought Dudley Tyler, the Hereford United winger who had almost sent them out of the cup back in February with his turn of speed and intelligent crossing skills. The other changes were the promotion of Pat Holland from three seasons as a sometime reserve up to first team midfield dynamo, and an inspired selection of the blond natural left-footed defender who had played in that FA Youth Cup game, Kevin Lock.

Geoff Hurst left Upton Park at the end of the season, aged 30, on a free transfer to Tottenham. Hurst had played in just three of the last fourteen league games that followed our FA Youth Cup victory at Upton Park, and I saw all three of them. He managed just one goal in those three games, a penalty in a 2-0 final day victory over Southampton, finishing his final season with a modest eight. Would he become the player I always felt he could have been at West Ham in his White Hart Lane twilight years? Would he link up again with Martin Peters to renew the fruitful partnership they'd enjoyed prior to the 1966 World Cup? The dulled grey eyes I had looked into at Upton Park back in February suggested otherwise.

West Ham started the 1972-73 season with a very different side to the one that had been relegated in 1971. It was still, in effect, Ron Greenwood's creation, but Cantwell had given it that twist of steel that meant Hammers would no longer be the first division's pushover boys. Or that was the theory. Forty-eight goals conceded over the season was a statistic that needed challenging. Bobby Moore wasn't anywhere near as quick as he had been in his younger days, but he was still good enough to play for and captain England, and with the youth of Lock to his left and the running of Bonds and Lampard to cover for him, it was a formation that had potential. Whether Bill Garner could make the step up from Southend United to perform to the demands of the first division remained to be seen. This was the team that Cantwell put out to start that season.

West Ham United 1972-73 First XI: Bobby Ferguson, John McDowell, Frank Lampard, Billy Bonds, Kevin Lock, Bobby Moore (captain), Dudley Tyler, Clyde Best, Bill Garner, Trevor Brooking and Bryan Robson, with Pat Holland as substitute.

The opening fourteen matches of that season chronicled a start that West Ham have never managed before or since. Noel Cantwell now had the balance of team exactly as he wanted it, and his gamble to give a first team place to England schoolboy international Kevin Lock was the most impressive of all. John McDowell and Bobby Ferguson were two average players who had been in the squad for some time, but they produced consistent performances throughout the early part of the season well above the standard previously expected of them. Billy Bonds and Frank Lampard stepped up to provide solid cover at the back, as well as furthering attacking options with some serious shooting power from distance. At 31 years of age, however, Bobby Moore was the most stunning of all, spraying 30 and 40 yard passes up and down the pitch at will to the feet of Tyler and Brooking, and keeping his players in check when the games got physical.

By the end of October, West Ham were five points clear at the top of the First Division, and even the early doubters in the press had been won over.

			F-A	
Aug 12th	West Brom (a)	W	1-0
Aug 14th	Coventry (h)	W	2-0
Aug 19th	Leicester (h)	W	6-1
Aug 22nd	Wolves (a)	W	1-0
Aug 29th	Liverpool (a)	W	2-1
Sep 2nd	Arsenal (a)	D	1-1
Sep 9th	Man United (h)	W	4-1
Sep 16th	Chelsea (a)	W	3-0
Sep 23rd	Norwich (h)	W	4-0
Sep 30th	Tottenham (a)	D	0-0
Oct 7th	Southampton (h)	W	2-1
Oct 14th	Ipswich (a)	W	1-0
Oct 21st	Stoke City (h)	L	0-1
Oct 28th	Man City (a)	W	3-0

		P	W	D	L	F	A	Pts
1	West Ham	14	10	3	1	30	6	25
2	Liverpool	14	8	4	2	21	12	20
3	Arsenal	14	7	4	3	24	16	18
4	Leeds	14	7	4	3	26	18	18

Goals: Garner 8, Robson 8, Best 5, Tyler 3, Bonds 2, Moore 2, Brooking, Lampard.

The only blemish on that opening three month sequence came towards the end of October, in a home game against Stoke City. With five successive victories at Upton Park, the team who were next to bottom of the First Division should have posed no problems at all.

It was a strange day all round. I was still playing for the Palace under-18s, even though I was already 18, and Chloe had met me at the ground that morning. She'd been up town and as we were going out that night, she said she quite fancied coming to see the Hammers play in the afternoon. This sudden bout of enthusiasm for football had clearly been fuelled by West Ham's early season success, but I didn't complain. She'd only been to Upton Park twice before in the previous season, and Hammers had lost both those games – to Chelsea and to Manchester United. I had banned her from going again, but relented this time mainly because of complacency about the opposition. A mistake.

It was the first game Bill Garner had missed since he'd joined the Hammers, the victim of a dead leg in training, so Pat Holland stepped up to wear the number nine shirt.

Hammers received the usual welcome from the crowd – they were now the only unbeaten side in the league – and they peppered Gordon Banks' goal with shots for the first twenty minutes, but the crossbar (twice) and the post kept them out. Then Banks stepped up, making three successive saves from Pop Robson that defied belief, the last one, diving backwards to fingertip a chip from the edge of the area over the bar, the best of the lot.

With ten minutes to go, the crowd began to disperse, sensing now that there wasn't going to be a West Ham goal. Then, in a rare attack, Stoke's Dennis Smith headed a simple sucker punch winner with a header at the far post from a late run, after some uncharacteristic lazy defending. It was their first away win of the season, and only their third win in six months!

In time I might have forgotten the game, but something happened the following day to etch it permanently in my memory. After a long lay-in round at Chloe's (her mum on holiday somewhere, as usual), I was downstairs getting something from the fridge when the news came on the radio. *Gordon Banks, the England World Cup Winning goalkeeper has been killed in a car crash just a few miles from his home. No-one else was seriously injured in the accident. Banks was pronounced dead at the scene after his car was said to have hit a tree. Tributes are already coming in from around the world ...*

It was a devastating piece of news. I felt oddly like a voyeur to have seen that game, his last game, and could still see the save from Robson, Banks' agonized expression as he stretched desperately in mid-air to deflect the ball over the bar. The save replayed itself in my mind all afternoon, and the news finally slowed the weekend to a virtual halt. In the end, I went home in the afternoon, something I would never ordinarily have done given the opportunity to spend it alone with Chloe. I wished, strangely, that I hadn't gone to the match, and I sat in my room for the rest of the day, quietly reading.

Hammers had a dip in form before Christmas, if you can call two further defeats a 'dip', but they started the New Year four points clear of the pack, which had now been joined by Derby County and Ipswich Town. It was a pleasant focus for me, while my so-called football career was on hold. Crystal Palace were top of the second division by eleven points and a certainty for promotion, it seemed. The Big Boss had begun to appear on television at the weekend, cultivating star status for himself as a football critic, cigar fiend and fashion oddball. He was now wearing a fedora, and had even sported a fur coat at a televised London premiere for the film *The Godfather* which he had somehow got himself invited to.

I hadn't seen anything of Charlie since he'd made his debut for Palace. He had played seven times for the club since August, four of them starts when he'd stood in for John Craven after the striker had a recurrence of an old knee injury. I'd felt strangely embarrassed for him, having to make it up with the Boss after such a public set-to, though I knew it wouldn't have bothered him. Charlie would do what Charlie wanted to, and through the stuttering start of what might still prove to be a brilliant football career, he was doing it.

I'd played a couple of games for the reserves, but it was well publicised that Palace were running the club on a shoestring, and with a first team squad of just nineteen, and a further ten not in either youth team, it wasn't unusual for there to be sixteen year olds in the reserves, some that weren't even on the club's payroll. It didn't make me feel particularly confident about my future in a football kit, but maybe promotion would change all of that. My only concern was to be given a proper contract at the end of the season, so I could allow football to become my means of employment for the next fifteen years.

Money was difficult. On one hand the banks were issuing 'credit cards' that allowed you to buy goods in shops and pay a bill to the bank the following month. On the other hand, still living at home and on a subsistence wage from Palace of just a tenner a week, I was struggling. I couldn't get any sympathy from dad – since the previous year's postal strike, he had become seriously politicised. He would attend TUC meetings and conferences every other weekend, as the 'strike that'll topple the government' that he had been talking about for over a year, drew ever closer. I hardly saw him from day to day.

My mother had also been politicised by the events of the last year, and had started to attend evening classes once a week while I babysat my sister. Everyone was getting on with their lives, improving themselves, taking on more issues in everything they did. Some mad sense of a need for self-improvement in the face of a developing social stagnation. And it hadn't exactly passed me by either. The country was going to the dogs. Everyone could see that. The threat of the IRA with bombs at the airport meant you weren't safe up town anymore. Unemployment was getting worse and money was scarce. Then there were the Americans who were not only still in Vietnam, but they had voted back in the idiot who had kept them there for the last five years. The previous Labour government, a left wing government, had actually supported the American presence in Vietnam, and the Tories of course continued the support. It seemed impossible that anyone could think it made any sense, but still it went on.

In the middle of all of this misery there was one beacon of light unexpectedly shining across the whole of London, its genesis in the small environs of Green Street, London, E17.

Noel Cantwell, the man who had replaced Malcolm Allison as West Ham captain in September 1957 and then led them to the 1957-58 Second Division Championship, had equalled that success by taking them to the Second Division Championship in his first season with them as manager, in 1970-71. Now, the unthinkable was suddenly up for grabs. In just two years, his side stood on the edge of winning their first ever domestic league title.

Bobby Moore, the man who Noel Cantwell had recommended to Ted Fenton back in September 1958 and who had become captain of the side himself in 1962 after Phil Woosnam had left for Aston Villa, this man was the key to it all. But West Ham wouldn't be the team they were if they had chosen to win the league at a canter. No – this was going to be a grandstand finish, and all the more desperate for me once it had become clear that Crystal Palace's second successive post-Easter slump had taken them out of the reckoning for promotion.

The 1972-73 season had seen West Ham dip twice – first just before Christmas (minor – two defeats in three) and second just before Easter (major – four defeats in five) when Liverpool and then Arsenal wrestled the lead from them. Two fantastic away victories over Everton and then Norwich City had thankfully taken them back up into first place.

As the last two games approached in the final week of April 1973, West Ham and Liverpool found themselves level on 58 points, with Arsenal third on 57. If it got down to goals, West Ham were always going to be the winners – they'd scored 76 goals! Liverpool had 67 and Arsenal 59.

The fixtures lined up thus:

	ARSENAL	LIVERPOOL	WEST HAM
Mon 23rd	Newcastle (a)	WBA (a)	Birmingham (a)
Sat 28th	West Ham (a)	Chelsea (h)	Arsenal (h)

West Ham had already lost at home to Birmingham City 2-0 in the middle of their second 'dip', both the goals being scored by Bob Latchford, whose brother David kept goal in the same side. West Bromwich Albion were bottom of the table, so looked a pushover for Liverpool, though Arsenal would struggle at Newcastle who had only lost once at home all season – to West Ham!

How odd.

St Andrews, where our makeshift Palace under-18 youth team had won in the FA Youth Cup last season, was the ground where West Ham had to win if they were going to give themselves a Championship chance on the Saturday.

I thought about Gordon Banks playing in that game at Upton Park back in October. He couldn't have known it was going to be his last, and yet he produced a performance that I and anyone who was there that afternoon would never forget. Just a silly football match, really. Why do we get so emotionally boiled over this crazy game? I knew then, as now, that what was to unfold over the next seven days, would immediately become a major piece of the weave of my strange life, however long it lasted.

Dave Spick phoned me at home late on the Sunday to get me to play in the under-18s Monday fixture. Two of his team had gone down with food poisoning on the Saturday – hardly surprising as they'd eaten a couple of the Selhurst Park chef's 'risky raviolis', a 'dish' that even Charlie, the human food dustbin, had always made a point of avoiding.

Despite the fact that the reserves were playing Reading on Wednesday, and I was supposed to be playing in that game, I had no choice. I would have to go.

I had managed to get a ticket for the Birmingham City game, so it wasn't a great moment in my life. The Birmingham game was taking place at the same time as ours, so how I would find out what had happened until the next day was anyone's guess …

As we ran out at Holmesdale, I was told that our opponents, Spurs, needed to win the game to keep their South East Counties Division 1 title hopes alive. All I knew previous to the game was that it wouldn't mean anything to the 'Young Eagles', who'd had another disappointing season. There were a few familiar faces in the team, notably Gary Bascombe who was even faster out of the blocks than he'd been last year. In the event we managed to hold Spurs to a 1-1 draw, thanks to a brave fighting display by a very young team, and my first ever goal for the under-18s, a tap-in after an unselfish cross from Don Edwards.

I had borrowed my mum's radio for the bus ride back, and after ascertaining that no-one on the bus knew the results (or anything about football, as it turned out), I went upstairs and began frantic efforts to tune into every single radio station, one by one, to find out what had happened. The first thing I gathered was the word 'disappointment' in a report about the West Ham game. I'd heard 'Birmingham City' but there'd been no mention of a score or of the Hammers, just some crap about how the referee 'had slowed the game down'. Then it began to come out in crumbs …

'the dismissal of McDowell'

'the Birmingham penalty'

'Latchford's first time effort … crashing back off the bar' (phew) …

So what about that 'penalty'? This was torture by subordinate clause.

'Agony as it sneaked just past the post …'

'a brilliantly timed tackle by Moore …'

'the second dismissal of the game …' (did we have two sent off?)

'the first time Latchford had been sent off in his career' (double phew)

'… in a desperately pressurised game'

'… incredible that it finished goalless …'

Goalless?

Pissballs.

If Liverpool had won, then it was out of our hands.

I hung on for what seemed like an hour.

In the end I missed my stop and found myself sitting outside the Dominion Theatre in Tottenham Court Road, clutching the radio. I couldn't get on the tube till I got the information I needed.

And after a horribly extended wait, it came in the next news bulletin, in simple scorelines with no frills. I held on. And finally five matches played this evening in the First Division. The scores finished:

Birmingham City 0 West Ham United 0;
Chelsea 4 Everton 0;
Newcastle United 2 Arsenal 3;
Stoke City 1 Ipswich Town 1;
West Bromwich Albion 1 Liverpool 1.

I waited for the brain fog to clear. What did that mean? Liverpool had drawn, so we were still level with them on 59 points, but Arsenal … Arsenal had won. They had won at St James' Park. How had they done that? Oh shit. Arsenal now had 59 points as well. All three of us on 59 points. It was going to the very last game of the season.

We couldn't rely on Chelsea doing us any favours at Anfield. The calculation was actually a very simple one. If we beat Arsenal, then we would bring the League Division One title back to Upton Park for the first time in our 77 year history.

CHAPTER SIX

Knowing Me,
Knowing You

I glanced over my shoulder at the sound of gravel under the slow tyres of the last car to arrive. As if the tension wasn't enough, she had decided to turn up after all. I squeezed my mum's hand in an effort to communicate the arrival. The priest waved at us and everyone moved slowly towards the chapel.

Just eight days after his fiftieth birthday, and my dad was dead. The show of family unity belied the events of the past two years since he had left us. He was the last man I would have thought capable of such an act. An overcertain man, a loyal man, a man not given to making mistakes ... He had returned one evening – a rare Sunday evening when we had all been in the house together – to make the announcement.

He had met her on one of his union weekends, up at Blackpool at a conference. Whether it was the pressure of events building up around him as a branch representative, whether he was ready for a belated mid-life crisis, whether marriage had simply become a lifeless matter of toeing the line – I wasn't actually interested any more. I just wanted to get this over with.

It was too clean a blow of retribution for him to be dead less than two years after that evening of revelations. None of us had really had the chance to let him know just how devastated we all were, especially Debbie, who was only seven at the time. I looked at her now, holding mum's other hand. She was too young for this. It might harden her up, make her angry. Time would tell.

I'd been awarded a contract at Palace, and had been thrown into the first team seven months later with the team struggling at the bottom of Division Two and no money in the kitty for new players. It was the day after I made my debut, at home to West Bromwich Albion, that dad came back to give us his news. He left an hour later, still ignorant of what I had achieved.

They say that life is all about timing, and maybe that's right. Why it is that I've ended up surrounded by so many people who've never heard the advice, or who have chosen to wilfully ignore it, I've no idea. He'd been there when it had all started for me. Came down to Palace once they'd talked about signing forms. Just hadn't been able to follow through. Union issues too important, then the postal strike, then get yourself a real job – once he realised I wasn't going to be another Jimmy Greaves. So there, dad. Look at you now. Just as well I stopped listening to you years ago.

I had my own place now. Even a Second Division footballer's wages could afford the one-bedroomed flat in Clapham that I was renting. I was just along on the tube from the old house if I wanted to pop home, and close to the training ground and Selhurst Park when I needed to be there. Palace had been relegated, but had come straight back up and were looking at possible promotion to the First Division once again.

Chloe and I had drifted apart a year back – I was in the Third Division and she had been promoted to the Major League European catwalk where she was swanning around, flashing off her legs for Gucci, Yves St Laurent and Hugo Fucking Boss. Relationships took time that I didn't seem to have, so they became something that I didn't seem to want. Charlie had been transferred to Manchester City, and had already found himself playing alongside former QPR favourite Rodney Marsh. Marsh had fallen into that predictable sporting lifestyle of the genius footballer who was always more comfortable on his laurels than in a tough game with the bar up. He had already been at Maine Road for one season and was regularly thrilling the crowds with skills that entertained, but that would never win prizes. Maybe that was enough – after all, wasn't football a game designed just to entertain? Its development into a serious money-making business over the latter half of the century could never have been predicted in the days of Burton Swifts and Northwich Victoria.

Malcolm Allison had somehow kept his job after Palace's relegation to the Third Division, but after some inexplicable forays into the world of soft porn and home furnishings, the Cuban Catastrophe was finally given the boot. His deputy, ex-Chelsea, Spurs and QPR midfielder Terry Venables, was popular amongst the players and supporters, and the obvious man for the reins after the Fashion Funny's departure. I liked Venables (though I wouldn't have asked him to recommend me an accountant) and the fact that he continued to pick me for the first team kept that relationship sweet for the time being.

Two weeks after dad died, Charlie unexpectedly invited me up to spend a weekend with him in Manchester. Palace didn't have a match as their opponents that weekend, Southampton, were in the semi-final of the FA Cup. Palace would have been playing them there themselves, had they been able to beat Chelsea in the quarter-final, but with our minds on promotion, the big ask remained just that throughout the game, and nothing more.

I hadn't seen Charlie since Palace had dropped to the Third Division, though I suspected his invitation had more to do with my dad's passing than it did with football.

I drove up on the Saturday morning, and went straight to Maine Road. Charlie had left me a ticket on the door and a pass for the players lounge after the game, where I was to meet him, Asa Hartford, Joe Royle, Colin Bell and a few other famous names now plying their trade at City. The opponents that afternoon were Ipswich Town who were sixth to City's ninth in the table. Whilst it wasn't exactly my choice of match, the form of both teams meant that it could be worth the price of the journey alone. Not only that, but though I had seen him a couple of times on television, it was actually the first time I had ever been to a game specifically to watch Charlie.

I was a little surprised that Charlie had chosen not to be around to meet me when I arrived, but had put it down to some match day routine that manager Tony Book was operating at the club. The seat they'd organised for me was in a perfect viewing position at the halfway line, and I found myself looking forward to the game as if I'd been at Upton Park.

The first disappointment was when I heard on the tannoy that Rodney Marsh wasn't playing, even though he was in the programme starting line-up. The second, and it was more of a shock than a disappointment, was when I caught sight of Malcolm Allison in the stand above, puffing away on a cigar and laughing at something the blond woman sitting next to him had said. I ducked my head down. I wasn't sure quite why I didn't want to be seen by Allison, but something intuitively told me my defensive response was a wise idea.

Charlie ran out in the number 10 shirt, which was the number Marsh had been wearing for most of the season. His name received a somewhat subdued cheer when it was called out by the PA announcer, the fans clearly anticipating Maine Road's 'main man' Marsh. Charlie had been playing in the number 8 shirt all season, but had given that up for the return of Colin Bell from injury. It might not have pleased him that Bell's announcement got the loudest cheer.

What was Allison doing here?

It wasn't a hard question to answer, on reflection. It was the club where he had built up his reputation as first team coach under Joe Mercer when City had last won the First Division Championship in the 1967-68 season, and the FA Cup two years later. He was still a hero at Maine Road, and as City hadn't won anything since, he was bound to receive a little hero worship outside and around the ground that might not go amiss. It was a better place for him to be than Selhurst Park, especially with Palace doing much better in his absence.

Ipswich started the game at a canter, and were ahead after just two minutes with a stylish goal from David Johnson, chipping the ball over the advancing Joe Corrigan from nearly twenty yards. City had saved their best form for the games away from Maine Road, and despite being in the top half of the table, had lost two of their three home games in March. This looked to be on their mind as they struggled to get back into the game.

Charlie had a shocker. Colin Bell also looked a little past his best, but still managed to put in a couple of good shots, and created a few chances for Joe Royle that went begging. Charlie was playing wide on the left, where Marsh had played, but though he had always been a versatile striker, he seemed strangely one-footed. The worst moment in the first half was when Asa Hartford picked him out with a 30 yard pass, and as he tried to feed Royle, he slipped and tumbled into touch and the ball rolled harmlessly through to the keeper. City were booed off the pitch at half-time, but even the booing was below par and the few hundred or so cheering Ipswich fans made the place sound more like Portman Road.

I stayed in my seat and peered up over my programme at the Upper Stand. Allison was laughing again. He was in a remarkably good mood for a man whose antics had made him a bit of a laughing stock. This was a man who was as likely to get a second job in management as

Charlie was to get a cheer when the teams came back out for the second half. I suddenly felt depressed. Wasn't I supposed to be enjoying this? Charlie had presumably had me come up here to see him play well and have a good time. As the former was looking unlikely, I'd have to work on the latter. I slunk out to grab a beer at the bar.

The queue reached back to the stand exit, but I joined it. If it was a choice of missing a beer or the start of the second half, it was no choice at all. As I stood in the queue, the half-times came over the tannoy. West Ham were beating Wolves 3-0. They hadn't scored more than two at home all season. Along with a mean defence, the goals had begun to dry up. Clyde Best had gone off to North America, along with many other players from the English First Division, including his namesake George. New leagues were being formed to try to help the game take off over there by a group of wealthy ex-pats who were cultivating some inexplicable vision of a motherland rebirth of colonial culture. Just how would they compete with baseball and American football? The other two strikers from that 'Greatest Ever' West Ham side, Bryan Robson and Bill Garner had left for Sunderland and Chelsea, respectively. Even in my own short life, I had witnessed some remarkable moments as a fan of West Ham United.

'Aren't you Roy Nolan?' a man said to my left. He was a City fan, wrapped in an overknitted white and light blue scarf, with thick glasses and a heavy northern accent that failed to explain how he knew me. I still nodded, though.

'I saw your goal against Swindon Town back in November last year. Goal of the Month it was.'

'Yes,' I said, unable to hide a smile at the memory. My only goal of the season at a game that ITV had decided to cover to avoid criticism that they only ever went to First Division grounds. We'd won the game 4-1, and my goal had been a thirty yard free kick that I'd only ended up taking because Peter Taylor had been injured in the first half. I had been practising them, however, and I caught this one perfectly, the ball cannoning into the Swindon net off the underside of the crossbar, which had added to the drama. Just why it had ended up Goal of the Month on ITV Granada's football programme, when the opposition that day wasn't even a Northern team, was one of the vagaries of sport on TV, which I'd never claimed to understand. After all, how could anyone explain why a national TV channel might want Malcolm Allison on their main regular football programme, mouthing off every week.

'Would you sign my programme?' the City fan asked.

'Sure,' I said, scribbling my looping monicker across, appropriately I felt, the programme's cover picture of Charlie Barth.

'Good luck,' he said, as he strolled off, clutching his programme as if it now might be worth something. Perhaps I should have asked him what he thought of Charlie's form this season.

The second half was a slight improvement, and though he continued to unimpress, Charlie ended up in the right place at the right time to tuck away an equaliser at the far post for City, with five minutes to go. The game finished 1-1, and I waited a few minutes for the crowd to disperse before going in search of the Players Lounge with my pass.

When I finally found the entrance, I balked at the density of smoke as the steward opened the door for me. I often smoked the odd cigarette, but my preference was very much for it to be genuinely 'odd'. This 40 a day habit that some of the pros maintained just made me short of breath, and as my pace covered a multitude of control sins on the pitch, I had to preserve anything that might keep it alive, like my lungs.

There were few players there yet, but Charlie had changed and was already at the bar, a cigarette in one hand and a beer in the other, chatting to the barman.

'Hi Charlie. Lucky goal.'

'Roy! How are you? Have a beer.'

Underneath the bonhomie, Charlie looked a little jaded, his eyes sunken, his pasty skin a cheap canvas for his grinning expression. We relocated to a quiet corner of the room.

'You playing number 10 now – where's Rodney Marsh?'

'Gone to the States,' Charlie said. 'Most players getting towards the end of their careers are moving out there. They reckon Marsh will be earning thousands in just a year. They have a different attitude to their sportsmen, out there.'

'You mean they pay them more, even if they're only playing a minority sport.'

'Women. Flash houses. Big cars. The States are putting a bid in to stage the World Cup Finals, so maybe that's behind it.'

I leant forward conspiratorially.

'So what's the Big Boss doing here?'

'Yeah, I was going to talk to you about that …'

I leant back again, and took a long swig on the beer.

'I'm listening.'

'I can't really talk about it here. Don't say anything. I'll tell you more later.'

We were two 22 year old kids from Hendon who had found ourselves in the second half of the twentieth century cast as professional footballers against a social backdrop of limited job opportunities and a less than certain future. Charlie's response was to enjoy whatever came his way, mine was less confident or decisive, a pondering outlook that had its roots in a different background.

We had another couple of beers and then drove across town to *The Racehorse*, a club owned by Mick Channon that Charlie seemed eager to spend time at. The beers had loosened me up and I was now ready for whatever the evening might offer, or thought I was, until we were greeted at the door of the club by a familiar face.

'Roy! My boy!' The Big Boss's familiar Semitic greeting was like an unexpected knife in the stomach. I felt my knees go weak, my brain transferring ideas to my legs before they could reach any other part of my body. I looked at Charlie and then I knew. I had naively thought I was here for old time's sake, to catch up with what had been. Instead, some other pre-meditated course of events was taking place, drawing me in without my volition.

The game is full of personalities – I'd always known that – but football, like any other popular enterprise where money is involved, is ripe for exploitation by the unscrupulous. Nothing succeeds like success, as West Ham had discovered, but they too had let it through their hands like sand, before they could get a real grip on it. Those with the biggest mouths maybe could, after all, speak louder than those whose talent had given them their platform.

Football was my life, and thanks to Geoff Hurst, the forgotten man, I had been able to make it a vocation. Driven by the force of injustices that he had suffered, I had come to worship that crazy team in the East End, and to play the game myself, at the back of my garden, honing my limited skills until they became something I could use on a full size pitch. I had worked on my belief as a player to improve my performances in the school team, until I had reached my goal of playing the game regularly to a good standard – until I had understood how to play, simply, and make the most of the limited talent I had. I honestly believe but for that inspiration, I might never have got to the stage where I could be recognised at a ground 200 miles from where I lived, and be asked for my autograph. Now I was there, now I could really call myself a footballer, where was my life heading?

As a fan, you have little control of what happens to your team, week in, week out. As a player, however, you can find yourself at the epicentre of its future. Your twists and turns, your runs and shots, your injuries and your spirit, these all have a very genuine effect on the fate of the team you play for. And what are the chances of a team finding eleven players who can all click on any one afternoon – or who can all click together more regularly in one season than any other team?

Back on April 28th 1973, West Ham United stood on the precipice of their greatest ever achievement as a football club. They knew moreover that they had to win just one football match to achieve it. The opposition knew also that they were at that same precipice, and defeat in the FA Cup Semi-Final to Second Division Sunderland earlier in the month meant they would be wanting it even more badly. Arsenal had not actually won the First Division Championship since 1953, and a win that afternoon would give them their first title for twenty years. West Ham, however, had *never* won the title.

When Arsenal were last Champions, the Hammers had been languishing in the Second Division, and had only avoided relegation to the Third Division that season by a mere six points. It would in all probability be less than a decade before Arsenal would have another shot at the title. We all knew as fans then that this might be the only chance that West Ham United would ever have. Which of the players could muster the necessary spirit to overcome the downside of whatever fate might throw at their side that afternoon?

West Ham United: Bobby Ferguson, John McDowell, Frank Lampard, Billy Bonds, Kevin Lock, Bobby Moore (captain), Pat Holland, Clyde Best, Bill Garner, Trevor Brooking and Bryan Robson. Sub: John Ayris.

Arsenal: Bob Wilson, Pat Rice, Bob McNab, Peter Storey, Frank McLintock, Peter Simpson, George Armstrong, Alan Ball, John Radford, Ray Kennedy, Charlie George. Sub: Eddy Kelly

I looked around the room at this club Charlie had seen fit to take me. He was at the bar with Allison, deep in conversation, shaking his head, before laughing. It was his fake laugh – easily spotted by the rasping breath that followed each ha-ha-ha – it hadn't changed in four years. It was actually his only laugh – when he genuinely found something funny, he just looked on, knowingly. No need to endorse.

This was the kind of situation I had often imagined as a boy – what it was like to be grown up – in an adult world, able to decode and decipher each glance and nod, able to make complete sense of everything, no matter what was thrown at you. Now I was there, I felt simultaneously baffled, thrilled, annoyed, delighted and yet stumped. How long would it be before I was given access to the kind of information that might be fissured with underlying danger like salmonella in an innocent slice of uncooked meat.

I looked up at a framed signed picture of one of Manchester City and England's greats, Francis Lee. There was a player still living his life to the full, a player who understood success.

I had got to the ground quite late that afternoon, considering the importance of the game, but the demands of an under-18 fixture had taken their toll on my day. I took up my position in the West Enclosure where I had relocated to in a season of West Ham football that had no equal. At the beginning of the season the fans had been saying it might be Bobby Moore's last year at Upton Park – the ensuing nine months had given the lie to that suggestion. Moore and Bonds, despite the latter's greater fitness, looked cut from the same cloth, and I sighed with pleasure at the moment – my team out there against the old enemy Arsenal, ready to do battle for the greatest football trophy there was.

Bobby Moore and Frank McLintock exchanged club flags in the centre circle in a short ceremony that would have had more meaning in an international tournament – perhaps that was the importance of the fixture in the eyes of the clubs.

John Ayris was sub that afternoon, replacing Holland who in turn had replaced the injured Dudley Tyler for his part in this afternoon of history that was about to be made, whatever the score. The rest of the side was fit, however – there was no real injury gripe for Cantwell – he had a quality side on show for the game of his managerial life.

Hammers kicked off, attacking the South Bank, and flew out of the traps, forcing three corners in succession. Brooking took the third which was headed inches wide by Kevin Lock.

Arsenal built their attacks more slowly, but were no less dangerous in their yellow change strip shirts and dark blue shorts, Alan Ball and George Armstrong littering passes around the ground and Kennedy testing Ferguson with two long range shots, hit with genuine venom.

Then the first fateful moment of the game. Charlie George was involved in a challenge with Bonds in front of the chicken run that forced George awkwardly to the ground. When he didn't get up, the Arsenal trainer sprinted over and began to look concerned. We didn't have a great view from the other side of the ground, but it was soon obvious that they were calling for a stretcher. Kelly was on after just twenty minutes, and it seemed as though Hammers had enjoyed a stroke of fortune that even the most sporting of fans can turn a blind eye to in a moment of need.

Should it have made a difference? Kelly was the perfect player to have on the bench, a workhorse – but not someone with the flair of George. Cantwell was yelling instructions to Bobby Moore that I couldn't quite pick up. The effect of the delay was seen on both sides as the game became scrappy and there were few chances before the half-time whistle. We heard over the tannoy in a rare announcement that Chelsea were 1-0 up against Liverpool at Anfield, Peter Osgood with the goal. If that remained the score, a draw with Arsenal would be enough. A win was preferable, but if a draw was enough then we'd take it.

I realised how dry my throat was – I had been yelling out encouragement to the eleven men out there in an attempt to sustain my part in swelling the Upton Park roar each time the Hammers burst past the halfway line. I did something I had never done before at West Ham. I went off to the bar to grab a beer.

The second half was mesmeric. The whole crowd was on acid. Claret and sky, white, yellow and navy. Had they put something in my beer?

I've always wondered about the power of the crowd to influence a game, those times when they seem almost able to will the ball into the net. But if there ever was one of those times, then this was it. The entertainers approaching their finest moment. Billy Bonds took a throw and found Moore on the halfway line, in space for the first time in almost a quarter of an hour. He looked up and hit the ball past the centre circle west to Trevor Brooking who dummied to let it run on to Pat Holland. Brooking's feigned turn was perfect as it took Bob McNab and Peter Simpson out of the play and left Holland with just Storey to beat. Somewhat predictably, Storey felled Holland like a sapling, on the edge of the box.

Before Arsenal could regroup, Brooking, who was right up with the play, chipped the ball to the far post where Clyde Best, not quite in position, threw himself at it, his efforts taking him smack into the club photographer by the advertising hoardings. Best's faint contact deflected the ball goalwards, looping it up over Wilson and over the bar. Or it would have done, if the spin hadn't held it in mid-air before carrying it unchallenged towards the goalline which it hit with a malignant magnetism before spinning backwards into the net.

The look on Pat Rice's face was an absolute picture. Arriving too late, McLintock kicked the ball with fury into the back of the net for the second time. A fluke? Maybe. Deserved? Certainly. Hammers had only been off the top spot for just three weeks all season, and had played as well as I'd ever seen them play. Arsenal were no slouches and wanted the win very badly indeed. They still had twenty minutes left, but it didn't make any difference. West Ham continued to attack, throwing all caution to the wind, with Bonds, Holland and Brooking nursing a midfield onslaught like an elasticated plumbline, until the right ball was created to send Robson, Garner or Best forward. Wilson, never a showy goalkeeper, played the game of his life to keep his side in with a late chance.

It was from one of Wilson's diving saves that Pat Rice gathered a loose ball, setting up a rare Arsenal attack. Kennedy raced into space on the right as Ball took the pass. His expertly judged flick would have sent Kennedy clear, but McDowell, very much an unsung hero over the course of the season, threw himself at it and cleared his lines. As the ball was pumped forward, Garner jumped with Simpson and won the aerial battle, his flick sending Robson through. Robson tamed the ball perfectly into his path before sending a shot all along the ground past Wilson into the corner of the net. The crowd lost control and invaded the pitch in their hundreds. Both teams ran towards the tunnel where they stayed, bunched around the dugouts, protected by a semi-circular line of yellow-coated policemen. It took five minutes for people to return to the terraces, but with just a couple of minutes to go, it didn't affect the outcome of the game, and referee Homewood's whistle began one of the most extensive afternoons of celebration that Upton Park had ever seen. Not only that, but within five minutes, there wasn't a single red and white scarf in the ground.

I swallowed hard, my throat sore with shouting. Looking down I saw that I had somehow spent the whole half holding on to my programme, now screwed up into the inverted shape of a clenched fist. The crowd were dancing up and down to 'Cum on feel the Noize', the song by Slade that had somehow taken over from 'Bubbles' as West Ham's anthem in their run in to this first ever title win. And you really could 'feel the noise' that afternoon as the crowd sang in celebration.

		P	W	D	L	F	A	Pts
1	West Ham	42	27	7	8	78	32	61
2	Liverpool	42	26	8	8	69	26	60
3	Arsenal	42	24	11	7	62	21	59
4	Leeds	42	22	10	10	58	38	54
5	Derby	42	22	8	12	70	58	52
6	Newcastle	42	23	5	14	66	44	51

The three photographs that capture that day perfectly are the first one, taken by the club photographer, of Clyde Best, having got the touch at the far post for his goal, with his arms outstretched as he over-balances towards the crowd. The expression of surprise is perfectly matched in his smile as he dives forward, desperately trying to stay on his feet. The second picture is of Pop Robson in the background, almost crouching, his eyes lit up as he watches his shot beat Wilson for the second goal. The ball is in the air, seemingly stuck to Wilson's fingertips as it evades them, bound for the corner of the net. The final photo is of Noel Cantwell addressing the crowd through the public address system. I can't even remember what he said – just the cheering, the cheering, which seemed to go on forever …

'Roy!' The throaty cockney voice brought me back to the moment as a pint of beer was almost literally shoved in my face.

'Careful,' I said. 'You'll have somebody's eye out. And mine's the only one it's near.' I was surprised at the deadpan sound of my voice. But then Allison was someone I hadn't spoken to in close proximity very often, despite being under him one way or another for most of my playing career.

'You don't look very pleased to see me.'

'How are you, Mr Allison?'

'Malcolm, please. Palace not playing today?'

'Our opponents Southampton are in the semi-finals of the FA Cup, as I'm sure you know.'

'Terry not got you in for training, then?' Charlie had joined us, but only just. He was a long way short of the kind of position that might suggest he had any part to play in this conversation.

'So what have you been up to?' I asked the question, though I didn't have any real interest in the response. Allison's pause and guarded expression made it clear that he hadn't expected me to be less than thrilled at him crashing in on my afternoon.

'I have a proposition to make, Roy. That's what this is all about. Players like you shouldn't be in the Third Division, should he Charlie?' Charlie smiled, but he also seemed a little uncomfortable. All Alison needed was his fedora and we'd be right back to the good old days. All there was in terms of trademarks was a cigar that he had put down in the ashtray in front of me.

'We might not be there much longer, the way things have been going,' I said. 'Bolton Wanderers and Bristol City have both lost their games in hand.'

'But the First Division, Roy. The fixtures, the crowds, you're in the shop window for your country if you hit a bit of form.'

'What's this all about, Charlie?' I said, trying to diffuse the monologue.

'Tony Book's done a good job at City since Joe Mercer left,' Allison went on. 'But this is a club that won the title and the FA Cup in the sixties. It hasn't seen any of that glory since then. What would you say about a chance to play for a team that was challenging for the title?'

It was predictable, but still a flattering offer. Was it real, though?

'I'm on a three year contract,' I said. 'Runs until August 1978.'

'Contracts can be broken.'

Once the agenda was clear and I'd declared an interest, the evening became a little more relaxed. The nature of the offer – the way it had been made – had all the hallmarks of Allison. *In absentia* from his chosen profession he had begun planning his next career move, playing on his fame as a boorish television football pundit, which was clearly some kind of takeover at Manchester City. I knew about his success there as coach to Mercer in the late sixties, but had no idea whether or not he still had anyone at the club who might want him back – let alone as the new manager. As for Charlie, who had hated this man more than anyone just four years ago, he seemed to have bought Allison's pitch. Why? Things looked good for him at the club – still able to enjoy a day at work even when he performed rather poorly. Why would he want to become part of something that looked decidedly shaky even before it had been proved possible?

These were questions that I got something of an answer to over the course of the evening. We left the club just after Allison and headed into town. Charlie had talked about *Loafers*, which was a celebrity hangout that was likely to offer its fair share of City and United players, as well as a few other surprises. United had got to the final of the FA Cup that afternoon, along with Second Division Southampton, so they'd be in a decent mood.

There was little visible in the city as we drove round to explain just why Charlie would want to stay there, however. Though it had only just turned eight, the streets were deserted.

'Once you know where everything is, it's a great place,' Charlie was saying.

'I don't see anything.'

'That's the point. It's not like London where you get mauled every time someone recognises you. You can move from place to place and stay out of the limelight.'

'Now why would you want that?' I said, mischievously.

'I like the limelight, don't get me wrong,' Charlie said. 'But I like to be in control.'

'So why shack up with Allison? He's the God of Control from what I can see. Hasn't changed a bit since his days at Palace.'

'That's where you're wrong, Roy. First thing I said to him when he came up here last month, was – what can you do for me? Seemed an obvious question. He said, what do you want? So I told him. And a week later, she's working at the club. That's the kind of influence he has. Do you see now?'

'Wait a minute – who's working at the club?'

'Suzy. Remember, that bird who used to work at Palace? Who you said I'd never go out with? She works at Man City now. In the ticketing department.'

I looked at him in disbelief.

'Yeah – I didn't believe it either, but right as rain, she turned up there the following week.'

'What a coincidence,' I said.

'Ah, but it's no coincidence. It's the way the man works. He gets things done – like he always has done.'

'He got Palace relegated,' I said. 'With the side we had that season, it couldn't have been easy. That was certainly impressive.'

Charlie pulled the car up outside a small hall that looked dead from the outside.

'And I suppose you've been screwing her ever since.'

'Nah,' Charlie said. 'No point. I just wanted to see if he could prove a point. And he did.'

'What about her?' I said.

100

'She's probably getting a decent wage. No point me losing any sleep over it, is there?'

Charlie got out of the car and I followed.

The surreal quality of the evening had just multiplied several times. There was something unpalatable about Allison, but something equally electric about his ability to 'make things happen', something almost erotic in his ability to move people around like they were pieces in a game of draughts.

This place was presumably *Loafers*, but it had a plain front, nothing on the outside to declare its contents. I recognised a couple of faces from the telly, middle aged entertainers drinking quietly at tables with girls who were either their daughters or women who valued fame and what it could buy above the appeal of simple logic.

I found myself thinking about my dad. What he had done had severed the connection on my moral compass. I knew it was going to be easy now not to care about any of this. I had felt remorse when Chloe had entered her own corridor in the world of money and fame, despite having some access there myself. I had felt angry and confused, but had never wanted to follow her. Just before Palace had been relegated to the Third Division, there had been some interest in me from Charlton Athletic, but I'd actually felt relieved when it had gone away. It had suited me to eschew any escalation in fame or success in football, unlike most of the players around me. Now I didn't really care. I was up for whatever might be about to happen. I could have driven home the minute Allison appeared on the scene, but maybe this was worth following through. I might learn something about what it was like to be a famous footballer; God, I might even learn something about myself.

'I know this bloke,' a sanguine face said in front of me. 'Goal of the Month, right? An unbelievable right foot, mate.'

'Hi,' I said. I didn't need an introduction. Not to this particular Liverpool legend, I didn't. And he knew about my goal!

'Roy's staying with me tonight,' Charlie explained.

'He's come to the right place,' said the Liverpool legend. 'Take it easy, though. Plenty left to enjoy tonight, but pace yourself.'

I wasn't sure what he meant, but when we stepped into the next room things became a little clearer.

'Get you a drink, Charlie,' one of the girls in front of us said. 'And your mate?'

'Two whiskies,' Charlie said. All four of the girls went off to get the drinks. It seemed a little excessive in terms of service.

101

'So one pours and the other holds while you drink?' I asked.

They'll all hold,' Charlie said. 'You'll see.'

It wouldn't be everyone's cup of tea, I was thinking. There would be footballers and entertainers who might prefer a night at home with the wife. Good luck to them. Except I was probably more like them than I was this particular brand of hedonists, with their doped-out smiles, frayed skirts and congealed make-up. Was this where most of those *News of the World* stories started – at clubs like *Loafers*?

I took a swig of the whisky and leaned back in the chair.

'You're a footballer, aren't you?' one of them said, in a heavy northern accent, probably Manchester. 'I could tell. You've got that kind of a body.'

I laughed at her line. This was going to be an interesting night.

CHAPTER SEVEN

Pride of London

It should've been the greatest moment of my life. I watched the giggling face of my two day old son as he stared up at me with genuine curiosity. No-one had ever looked at me like that before; man or woman, adult or child. It was a unique feeling. Today was Wednesday 2nd April 1980.

We'd married in October, but you wouldn't have known the full story even if you'd been there. There were friends and family surprised at the speed of it all, but then I'd always done things my own way, made my own decisions without consulting others ... at least since my father's death. No-one should have questioned the path I'd chosen, and few did to my face until January, when certain physical appearances finally satisfied the wanton speculation that had been hanging around like a cynical relative waiting for someone to die.

I'd always wanted to do things right in my life. I had made mistakes, particularly the eighteen months spent at Manchester City, but coming back to Crystal Palace in early 1978 had been a good move, especially once we'd been promoted the following season. As for my personal life, leaving Manchester had meant finally kicking some bad habits I'd got into. Unthinkable, some of them. The main ones were shagging anything with a pretty face and drinking any strong alcohol I might find in a three inch glass. The souped-up Capris and gambling club venture completed the full house of clichés, and had left me spending my first year back in London paying it all off.

I had felt numb most of the time, if I felt anything. The game had changed and maybe the players had changed with it. For a long time, the game was all I had. The thrill of the day of a game, waking up that morning, knowing that what you did on the pitch that afternoon would be in the record books for ever. It might simply be another appearance against your name – it could be a goal, even a sending-off, but it would be instant history, immute and unchangeable.

Few of the players I knew now felt that way about it. To them it was just a game, a highly-paid profession that they would make as much money out of as they could while the opportunity was there. Most of them couldn't tell you much about their career beyond the season they were playing in. I was different. I may have wasted a lot of my life up in Manchester, but I could tell you the statistics on the pitch. 1976-77: 27 starts in the league, 3 substitute appearances, 2 goals. 2 League Cup, 1 FA Cup, no goals. 1977-78: 23 starts in the league, 4 goals. 1 League Cup appearance, 1 goal. Overall 57 appearances 7 goals. Despite that, there are still fans up there who won't remember me, even though my last game was only two and a half years ago. They can say what they like, but they can't argue with the record books. It's there forever now.

And my son, Geoff – that's what we're going to call him. He's in the record books, too. There's no changing that either, even though I sometimes think … You're bound to. Even when you know it's wrong. But it's not his fault.

I met Gary Bentley when I was up in Manchester with the Cuban Cartwheeler, deep in some shit or the other. Gary was in the Leicester side we'd just drawn 2-2 with, and he had remembered me from a FA Youth Cup game at Birmingham a few years earlier. Said I'd been 'this scary six footer' who'd given him the run around that night at St Andrews. I didn't remember him from the game, but as he'd given me the run around at Maine Road that afternoon, or had been impossible to get past at least, I decided I'd have a drink with him.

Turned out we had plenty in common, coming from similar backgrounds – though he was from Bromsgrove – and he told me about how he'd been doing this FA coaching course to qualify for management. It seemed a little premature as he was only in his mid-twenties, like me, but it still made a lot of sense. Few players got beyond their mid-thirties when they finished their careers, and there was precious little to move on to vocationally, apart from writing a salacious book of memoirs or becoming an opinionated football pundit. With no current plan to do either, I began thinking about what it might be like to pass on my experience. Reflecting on the managers I had worked with, and those I'd seen at West Ham United, I could imagine how it might be done well. I had worked perhaps too long with Malcolm Allison, who was still a very good teacher of what to avoid getting involved with as a manager. Then there was Terry Venables, who I was still with at Palace, one of the best, and a man who managed to juggle the skills of being a good man manager with being an excellent communicator, so always able to conduct himself perfectly with the media, saying just enough to say what he meant and not so much to sound like he didn't mean what he said.

Over the next few months I built up a close friendship with GB, as I came to call him, and it was the first time that I had thought with balance about a future after football. Playing it at least.

One man who had surprised me with his managerial skills was Johnny Lyall. Taken under the wing of Ron Greenwood – though it wasn't exactly well publicised at the time – John had played for West Ham until an injury had forced him out of the game in 1963, but he had remained on the staff and had always taken a great interest in coaching, even when he was still playing the game. When Noel Cantwell took over at West Ham, he took Lyall on as his deputy, and has given Lyall great praise since for his part in the training and preparation of the 1972-73 Championship side. Lyall took the position of joint manager with Cantwell in August 1976, finally taking the job over fully in February 1978, with the side at the bottom of Division One. It was a brave move, and with the subsequent news that there was no money for new players, he found himself presiding over West Ham's first relegation since 1969-70, three months later.

Lyall could still call on the services of Trevor Brooking and Billy Bonds, even with the Second Division looming, but that side was very different to the one that had won the Championship back in April 1973, five years previously. Bobby Moore had gone to Queens Park Rangers for the last two seasons of his career, almost taking them to the title in only their third season in the First Division in 1976. Best had gone to America to New York Cosmos, Robson to Sunderland and Bill Garner across London to Chelsea, who had been relegated in his first season with them. McDowell and Lock had gone to Fulham and Frank Lampard had been forced to retire prematurely as a result of a serious hip injury. The pluses were Mervyn Day's continued agility in the West Ham goal, and Alan Devonshire, surely the find of the decade, signed from non-League Hayes, and already a regular in the England U-23 side.

For the first time in my life I found myself playing football in the league above West Ham. I had turned out just once for Manchester City against the Hammers under Allison in the First Division, in a game at Maine Road that City had won 3-2. Brooking scored and made both West Ham goals, but this was when Brian Kidd had come to City and was in an unstoppable run of form. His two goals and a Tommy Booth late winner had grabbed the points. I got clobbered by Billy Bonds on a run down the left wing in the seventh minute, and wasn't really the same for the rest of the match, despite an adrenalin rush that had me running round the pitch like a pigeon with no head. This was during a lean period for Charlie when he'd fallen out with Allison – again – and had subsequently been dropped. He did eventually get back in the first team, but only after I'd left.

I'd had four chances to play against West Ham, but with one thing and another I only got the one opportunity. It was one of those strangely elusive fixtures, as I never did get to play at Upton Park in a Manchester City shirt.

John Lyall would have to work miracles to do something constructive with the West Ham side he had been left with, and he knew that any success he achieved would be down to him and him alone. Rarely can that have been said of many managers in the English Football League.

The season taking West Ham United into the eighties is already looking like the one that will put the past behind them. Although the seventies produced West Ham's first ever championship side, it also saw the Hammers relegated twice. Despite that, in Lyall's second full season in charge, he has already overseen the side's best cup run since they were knocked out by Arsenal in the quarter-finals at Highbury in March 1975. Looking at the side he's built since, demonstrates his architectural skills as a manager, bearing in mind the detritus he was originally left with.

West Ham First XI (1979-80): Mervyn Day, Ray Stewart, Mark Dennis, Billy Bonds, Alvin Martin, Alan Devonshire, Pat Holland, Geoff Pike, David Cross, Trevor Brooking, Paul Hegarty. Sub: Paul Brush.

To have picked up Hegarty and Stewart from Dundee United was a remarkable double signing, strengthening the defence and the attack in one shrewd piece of business. Londoner Mark Dennis looks as good a left back as I've seen for some time, and David Cross has proved a handful for defences in the Second Division. Not only that, but now Lyall has taken West Ham to the semi-finals of the FA Cup for the first time since they won the trophy back in May 1964. As a Second Division team they are naturally seen as the underdogs, but they can beat anyone on their day, and maybe Ipswich Town, despite their First Division pedigree, won't prove too great an opposition. If Hammers get past that obstacle, there's the promise of Arsenal or Liverpool in the final. Quite a challenge.

Despite the quality on paper of his first eleven, Lyall has failed to get promotion for the second year running. Sunderland and Birmingham City are fighting it out for the title, while Chelsea and Queens Park Rangers are just behind them, but ahead of West Ham. Bizarre to think that all those teams were in the First Division just a few years ago.

Sometimes I still think football is all I have.

'Are you still here?' she says.

'Yeah, thought I'd hang around until you woke up.'

'Are you coming over this weekend?'

'Yeah.'

'Roy …?'

'Look, I don't want to talk about it. Just let me have some time on my own. I'll be round on Sunday. So long as you make sure no-one else is there. I've got to go now …'

'Will you ring me?'

I don't reply to the last question. I'm already out of the ward and away down the hospital corridor, away to a place where I can think straight.

The problem doesn't have any obvious immediate solution. It's not about what she did. I'm past that now. I was even past it before we got married. It's the fact that the fucking kid could belong to any one of the three of us. Three of us! One doesn't know and the other one is praying there weren't too many in the deep end when he dipped his wick. Actually, it could've been any one of four, but then the colour of the baby has ruled the last one out.

There are bound to be those who blame me. Her mother, for example. She knows the whole story. I asked Vivien to keep it quiet, to say we'd had second thoughts and got back together for the kid, but it was too late. She'd already explained what had happened. How I'd finished it and told her I'd got back with Chloe. How I couldn't see her any more. How she'd then gone on a South London man binge, collecting bodily fluids from anything in trousers. How she was now pregnant –

107

what did anyone expect? How one of them was an American, Tony, she met in a bar, who lives in Minnesota, and who she doesn't even have any contact details for. How the other is an unemployed friend of her brother's, Simon, who she's had an on-off relationship with, mostly off, for years. The man from Westbourne Park, like I said, he's out of the picture now.

I want to be magnanimous about it. After all, I shagged enough women in Manchester to have fathered a couple of football teams. Genetically speaking, my Northern efforts might even have provided the raw material for a decent match, but the point is I knew what I was doing. Or put it another way, I knew at the time that I was travelling through a dislocated part of my life. I took precautions. Mostly. And when I didn't, there were reasons for it that made some sense.

Simon knows it might be his. Thankfully he doesn't look like Bela Lugosi, but he does have distinctive features, features that I've often thought of dislocating out of all recognition. Features that I may soon be seeing closer to home than I'd like.

Vivien and I had actually been out together for nearly a year, but it wasn't the kind of relationship that had any future in it. Or it shouldn't have been. Thinking back, it wasn't as if there was anything to suggest we might one day have something in common bar the kind of pent-up lust that could be bottled and sold like deodorant. That bit I do remember. And still remember. It's a memory that's stored in places other than my brain. Uncomfortable as it is to recall, she fucked like no-one I'd ever been with. Everything. Every which way. My drained thoughts on that first night were that she must be the one. It was as though some-one had cleared out my gonads with a wire brush. I was truly spent, in every sense. Spent of vision, and judgement too. When I see her now, there is a thin refracting film between me and her that presents a sub-tly different picture. The visual information that previously triggered every particle of lust in my body has been airbrushed out. I see instead the crossply woman I married last October, the mother of my child, a child herself, dependent, irrational and desperately lonely.

Vivien's mother is like a grown up version of her daughter. Grown up by about another eighteen months. She begins all her sentences with the word 'but'.

'But someone has to provide for him …'

'But you were the one who called it off …'

'But I'm only trying to be a good mother, a good grandmother …'

But but but but …

Even this would be bearable if I hadn't met Chloe last August, coming back from the pre-season tour to America with Crystal Palace. As a kind of reward for our promotion success in 1978-79 (and, more importantly, as a positive financial statement to the fans about the club's new owner) Venables had utilised his contacts with Rodney Marsh to set us up with a North American tour. I'd played three halves of the four games, and was flying back early to receive some treatment on my right ankle. Venables had sent me back first class, which meant I would be rubbing shoulders with a crowd of social worthies. I wasn't protesting.

Chloe Shrimpton was now a top model at the height of her fame, the face of perfumes and impossible ranges of clothes with price tags that could make your wallet sweat. I had come to enjoy seeing her in advertisements on television and in magazines, remembering the years we'd spent together. When I saw her in the aisle opposite mine, there was nothing for it but a double take. The fact that she immediately smiled and came across to see me, quashed any cynical fears I might have had time to organise.

'Roy? The famous footballer!' She laughed, but with the smile that I remembered from a Sunday afternoon long ago. I looked at her, rather longingly I felt. I stated the obvious.

'You're one to talk about fame!'

'But I saw you at Chelsea, playing for Manchester City, when was it – must be over a year ago?'

That'll be the Peter Osgood connection, I found myself thinking.

'I'm back at Palace now. We're in the First Division!'

Chloe smiled, but this time without understanding. She loved the combative essence of football, but taking her beyond the simplicity of two teams head to head on a pitch into the whys and wherefores of promotion, relegation and – God forbid – the offside law, and you might as well enrol her in a ten week Quantum Mechanics course, for all the sense she'd get out of it.

'Don't sound so surprised. I always knew you were going to make it.' She let her hand drop slightly, so it brushed mine, and I pushed my fingers forward to hold it. It felt delicate, sensitive and a little cool against the heat of mine.

'It really is good to see you,' I said, finally, to punctuate the hanging moment.

As it happens, in what is to be the first FA Cup Final of the 1980s, West Ham United, little West Ham United of the Second Division, are in the

FA Cup Final for the first time in 16 years. The team that got to the semi-finals of the European Cup back in 1974, have finally put together an unstoppable run of cup games that means they will be at Wembley on Saturday 10th May. It's still not clear whether they'll be playing Arsenal or Liverpool (who are already into their second semi-final replay), but they are already there, and thanks to Gary (and his connections at the FA) I have a guaranteed ticket.

Their route to the final is a rather bizarre one:

			F-A
FA Cup R3	West Brom (a)	W	2-1
FA Cup R4	Leyton O (a)	W	4-1
FA Cup R5	Swansea (h)	D	2-2
FA Cup R5R	Swansea (a)W	W	2-1
FA Cup QF	Aston Villa (h)	D	0-0
FA Cup QFR	Aston Villa (a)	W	3-2
FA Cup SF	Ipswich (Villa Pk)	W	2-1

It doesn't take a genius to spot what is odd about this cup run. In that season, Hammers could not win at home in the cup to save their wives. They nearly lost against Swansea City, only saving the game in the last five minutes, but the really remarkable game was that Upton Park Quarter Final against Aston Villa where Ray Stewart, who had never missed a penalty for West Ham, had the chance to win from the spot in the very last minute after a Villa handball from a corner, forced by a great run from Alvin Martin.

Stewart, who is nicknamed 'Tonka' because of the way he blasts his penalty kicks, unaccountably decided that day to sidefoot the ball past Jimmy Rimmer, and though he beat the keeper, the ball came back off the post and was cleared by a Villa defender. Five of the West Ham players had turned their back on the kicker, unable or unwilling to see the fate of Tonka's effort. The disappointing groan of the crowd soon made the result clear. Incredible that they should then fight back so brilliantly at Villa Park after being two goals down in five minutes to finally win the game a minute from time, thanks to Ray Stewart's old Dundee United teammate Paul Hegarty arriving late at a Geoff Pike corner to power the ball home on the volley. It was a remarkable goal, not just because of its timing in the game, but also because of the way Hegarty leapt off the deck to hit the ball in mid air with all the power he could muster. It was a goal that they would talk about for many years

110

to come, the goal that put West Ham in their first FA Cup Semi-Final for 16 years.

The route through to the final was a lot more comfortable than the quarter-final had been. Though Ipswich Town were at the top of their game that season under Bobby Robson, in the UEFA Cup and lying third behind Liverpool and Manchester United, they were in a league that included Brighton and Bristol City. This was when, with a few notable exceptions, the First Division was full of teams that should have been in the Second Division, and the Second Division was full of quality teams like West Ham United (and the others I've mentioned) that should've been back in the first.

When they had increased the number of teams involved in promotion and relegation from the First to the Second Division to three, this was always what was bound to happen. If only Lyall could have secured that last promotion place. In the event, Hammers could still be satisfied with an FA Cup Final, and a chance of European Football, even as a Second Division side, if they won it. They could even get there as losers, as Arsenal (if they beat Liverpool) were contesting the 1980 European Cup-Winners Cup Final against FC Valencia in the Heysel Stadium, Brussels, the following week, and would qualify automatically as holders if they won it. West Ham couldn't take that chance, though – they had to win.

The semi-final against Ipswich Town was played at the traditional neutral venue – in this case Villa Park, where West Ham had, by coincidence, already won their quarter-final. This seemed a stroke of luck to the Hammers, players and their fans alike, being the superstitious lot that they have always been.

On the day of the semi-final, Ipswich Town seemed to have their minds elsewhere, and capitulated to two quick goals before half-time, the first from David 'Psycho' Cross, so-called because of his uncanny resemblance to Anthony Perkins from the Hitchcock thriller of the same name, quickly followed by another typical drilled volley from Paul Hegarty.

It's said that one of the best times to score is just before half-time, as it is guaranteed to have a profound effect on the substance of the other team manager's half-time pep talk. The manager may lose it with his team and start screaming and yelling – never a great motivator when you're amongst grown men. Then he may decide paradoxically not to overreact, as he sees it, and end up making his players feel he doesn't care about the match. Mixed messages at such a crucial time in a game

111

can only weaken any chance the side might have of getting back into the game after the break.

In West Ham's case, Hegarty's second goal all but sealed the game. Hammers' defence had not got through any of the previous rounds without conceding a goal, and Johnson's reply, early in the second half, made Lyall decide to bring on Paul Brush to replace young Paul Allen, and give the defence added options. They didn't need them. Ipswich faded in the second half and Hammers ended the game as worthy winners. Ipswich Town had won the cup two years earlier, but they weren't going to win it this year.

After meeting Chloe on the plane, I realised that I had been premature to compartmentalise our relationship as just a small part of my growing up. She was sophisticated, a little untouchable perhaps, at first glance, but I felt comfortable with her. The petty jealousies I could have rightly been accused of on many occasions, seemed to have disseminated.

She was blissfully ignorant of the irrational enmity I had felt towards her in all the time I hadn't been seeing her. She clearly had no idea how I had felt. There was something to be said, then, for keeping things to yourself; for being, in bellybutton parlance, an 'inny' rather than an 'outy'.

Chloe had given me the phone number at the flat she shared with her friend Jenny, another model, although she said between them they were probably only ever there for one week out of every four. She made a point of writing the number on a promotional scented Chanel card with her photograph on the front. On many occasions before I finally summoned up the courage to meet up with her, I ran my nose across its edges, imagining the fragrance along her shoulder above the soft skin on her neck. Even at arm's length she still smelt breathtaking on the plane that evening.

Settling back in London after Manchester had taken no time at all. I had kept my Clapham flat, renting it out fairly cheaply to one of my cousins. Her legendary fastidiousness meant that I was receiving an income from it in addition to securing its maintenance throughout the whole period I was out of town. Classic planning.

I had known Manchester City would never be a long career stop, but hadn't actually planned on coming back to Crystal Palace. My signing was one of those low key end of season stocktaking deals that is kept clear of the media, whilst still proving financially astute for all those involved. Away from the easy lifestyle I had enjoyed around the different suburbs of Manchester, I had become a little more focused and level-headed. The delight of free-fall for me had never meant taking my eye off what kind of landing might be ahead. The bad habits began to look less like lifestyle choices and more like simple bad ideas. Once Allison's short reign had ended, Charlie found that he was now just a well-paid squad player, making twenty or so appearances a year, and all this before he'd even got to 26.

My career, however, had blossomed, and I was now the first choice number 8 for Crystal Palace as they came to the end of their first full season back in the First Division. It was still a struggle, though, and we had hovered around in 15th position for most of the season. These were great days for Palace, with the likes of Kenny Sansom, Gerry Francis and Jerry Murphy all playing out of their skins every week for the Eagles.

The most memorable incident that season for me, as a player, was when we went across to play Norwich City in February, and I met Ron Greenwood after the game. Ron had remained in football after being sacked by West Ham at the beginning of the seventies. He had gone on to manage Leicester City to promotion, and then emulated his achievements at Norwich City, who were now an outfit able to hold their own in the upper half of the First Division. I didn't get the chance to speak to Ron, but sat in on a conversation between him and Terry Venables in the bar after the game. It was interesting how the two men, who had both played for Chelsea in their careers, obviously had a strong mutual admiration for each other's style of management, and the topics they discussed that evening would have probably merited a major newspaper article on the future of football.

Despite West Ham's Championship success in 1972-73, the fact that they had been relegated just a few years later made Greenwood's promotion seasons at two clubs with fairly empty trophy cabinets to date look particularly impressive. Greenwood hadn't ever had to return to the Second Division once he left Upton Park, and at the ripe old age of 58, had already taken Norwich City to promotion and to the League Cup Final, which they had won against Aston Villa in 1978, 1-0. In addition to that, Greenwood's Norwich beat Palace that afternoon 3-1, all the goals from signings he had made in ex-Hammer Martin Peters (who he had signed from Spurs), Mark Barham (up through the ranks) and Alan Taylor, a top striker Greenwood had picked from out of nowhere, signing him from Rochdale in 1973, for a pittance.

When I finally contacted Chloe after the meeting on the plane, I decided that we should meet up somewhere special. It might have made more sense just to invite her round to my flat, but to avoid looking predatory, I picked *Mongrels*, a jazz club in Croydon some of the less rowdy elements of the squad at Palace had picked out for its good music and excellent food. The club was owned by Ronnie Scott, and as a result, often featured unbilled stars from the world of Jazz who would pop in and play a quick set after an evening playing in Greek Street.

Chloe's flat was in Charlotte Street, a lot nearer *Ronnie Scott's* than *Mongrels*, but she agreed to meet me in Croydon on the evening of the penultimate Saturday of the season. Palace had beaten Middlesbrough 1-0 at Selhurst Park, and were more or less guaranteed to finish 13th, our best league placing ever, and I was part of the Eagles team that was about to secure that achievement.

The success of football in the sixties, since the World Cup win, had led to a plethora of clubs and bars to cater for those whose lifestyles had generally given them an inverse proportion of money to common sense. These were the kind of places where footballers and the famous who wanted to hang out, hung out. The different people you might meet there meant that any evening offered potential surprises, but I had found that the more rich and famous someone was, the more unapproachable they were likely to be, even in the company of the equally rich and famous.

Mongrels wasn't just a meeting place. Unlike the formica tables and plastic tablecloths at *Ronnie Scott's*, *Mongrels* had been furnished with solid dark wood tables and benches, low cream lighting fixtures and ergonomically designed steel tubed black leather chairs that seemed like giant hands eager to cup your buttocks. The waiters were a mix of men and women, invariably Spanish or American – or both – who moved noiselessly around, locating orders and fetching drinks. The walls were all varnished dark brick, adorned with metal framed photographs of all the Jazz Greats: Louis Armstrong, Count Basie, Billie Holliday, Chet Baker, Ella Fitzgerald, Miles Davis, Thelonius Monk and Charlie Parker – those are just the ones I can remember. When you looked more closely, you saw that these weren't actually photographs, but brilliant evocative drawings of the artists at play, caught midstream making music.

Unfortunately there was invariably a feeling that over half the people there were there in spite of rather than because of the music. Some even complained that they couldn't hear themselves speak. It was just a neat place to grab a few beers until you moved on – not everyone ate there. Most of the Palace crew didn't enjoy or even know much about

114

Jazz – music for them was mainly pop, reggae or what was these days known as 'New Wave' – the Jam, the Clash and the Police. I felt a bit like my dad must have, being out of step with modern tastes. When I came to the club, I usually stayed until 2am and got a taxi back if we weren't training the next day.

I hadn't even finished my first beer when I looked up from my table and saw Chloe. There was only one word for it – fuck. I hadn't ever seen her look better – a long black dress under a roll of blonde hair and a single silver necklace. She sat at the bar, low key, chatting to the barman who was laughing at something she had said. I watched her for a good couple of minutes, prolonging the moment when she would see me, ready to enjoy it. When she ran out of visual stimulus and turned into my line of vision, I laughed. What a clown! She threw her arms to the sky, feigning an exaggerated expression of amused disbelief, before turning back to take her drink and cross the room to where I was sitting.

'Why do they call it *Mongrels*?'

'Don't ask me,' I said. 'I just spend money here.'

'I thought it meant mixed breed.'

'I didn't ask you if you liked Jazz.'

'What's that got to do with it?'

'Everything. That's what this club's about. Jazz. A mixture of all the music in the world. Something for everyone. I don't understand it, but I like it.'

'I don't understand you,' she said. 'But I like you.'

'What's there to understand?' I said.

Ever since seeing *Annie Hall* I had wanted to have the lines that Woody Allen writes, to have them pop up into my head at will. Being with Charlie had sharpened my desire for a quick answer. What Charlie lacked in brain, he more than made up for in repartee. When I tried to do it, it just sounded corny.

I didn't feel a need to be clever with Chloe. Travelling around Europe she had seen plenty, and would always be more likely to be impressed by nature than cultured artifice. I listened to her stories about people whose names I knew well from magazines and television, about how everything her aunt had told her about the business was true, about how she simultaneously loved and despised what she did. There was now a desire from the world of fashion – possibly out of guilt – to be seen to be somehow more than just show. To champion causes, put money and time into the needy in Africa and India. It sounded worthy, but at the same time strangely shallow. The reason had to be right. I was also beginning to care about bigger issues than just who might make the first team next week.

The likelihood in the UK was that there would soon have to be another general election just twelve months after the last, and with things not much better than they had been the year before, it looked like the Conservatives might get in. That would put the kybosh on the weak and needy. Jim Callaghan and David Steel's resurrected Lib-Lab pact had never looked more fragile. All the newspapers were gunning for 'Uncle Jimmy'. Why should I care? I couldn't remember any politician making a difference since Winston Churchill, and there were now even several contradictory assessments of his days in office. It would always be easy for the footballers and the models. Maybe it was time for worthy issues. Chloe seemed to think so, anyway.

If the evening had disintegrated spectacularly, as many of my Manchester dates had throughout my time up there, things might have progressed more comfortably in other areas of my life. As it was, I had one of the most memorable evenings I would ever have. The food was perfect, I maintained a spirit level sainthood between sobriety and recklessness, and Chloe was lovely. When it seemed as though things couldn't go any better, the club manager Steve introduced a special guest jazz trio who'd been taxied over 'fresh from Ronnie's to entertain a top South London crowd'. Two wiry teenage dinner jacketed musicians took the stage, one on double bass, the other drums. They looked like the kind of kids you might see outside on the street on your way in, but the moment they started playing, it was clear that they were at the top of their game. The third member then took to the stage, a well-built man comfortably old enough to be grandfather to the other two, with a barely perceptible smirk on his face. In spite of his heavy build and large hands, when he touched the piano keys, hitting just a few notes, it was unmistakably him, the great Canadian man of Jazz. How many people in the world could hit a few notes on a piano and announce their arrival in a room so unequivocally?

I checked my watch. 1.30 am.

'Oscar Peterson,' Chloe whispered in my ear.

I nodded, gleefully.

On Saturday 10th May 1980, West Ham United came out at Wembley in front of 100,000 spectators and all the pomp and ceremony that the occasion produced. They'd been there in 1964, but as a nine year old blind to the lure and passion of association football, the occasion had passed me by. That afternoon, freed from the restraint of performance, I could watch the game as a boy, spellbound by the occasion, hypnotised by the crowd and the fanfares, incandescent with hope for the success of my team.

Every football fan should have the chance to see their team compete at such an occasion. It is, in addition, a rare opportunity for outsiders to understand the appeal of football to a committed spectator. People complain that too many cup final tickets are given away to people who have no love or knowledge of the game, let alone heartfelt support for either of the teams playing. It would have been hard for anyone, fan or neutral, to have been at the ground that day and not to have felt privileged to be part of an atmosphere unparalleled in any sport in this country.

Arsenal had finally got through to the final after a third semi-final replay over Liverpool. If West Ham could beat them as underdogs after their struggle to reach Wembley, so much the better. The main significance of Arsenal as opposition beyond the fact that we all hated them was that this was only the second ever cockney cup final in the competition's history. In the other one, Spurs had beaten Chelsea 2-1, back in 1967.

The Cup Final teams that John Lyall and Terry Neill led out that afternoon promised a memorable match, with Arsenal more than keen to seek revenge for their Football League title decider defeat at Upton Park back in April 1973. Hammers were missing only Mark Dennis from one of the best Second Division sides not to be promoted from a season's football in the history of the Football League. Dennis's broken ankle, sustained after a vicious two-footed tackle from Archie Gemmill of Birmingham City just three weeks previously, would keep him out for at least four months.

West Ham: Mervyn Day, Ray Stewart, Paul Brush, Billy Bonds, Alvin Martin, Alan Devonshire, Paul Allen, Geoff Pike, David Cross, Trevor Brooking, Paul Hegarty. Sub: Pat Holland

Arsenal: Pat Jennings, Pat Rice, Sammy Nelson, Brian Talbot, David O'Leary, Willie Young, Liam Brady, Alan Sunderland, Frank Stapleton, Steve Walford, Graham Rix. Sub: John Devine

Gary had got both of us terrace tickets (at my request) behind the goal that West Ham attacked in the first half, but there were no goals to be had in that first frantic 45 minutes. Arsenal looked a little shell-shocked after their semi-final marathon with Liverpool, and it was nearly twenty minutes before they were even able to produce a shot on goal. West Ham had two excellent chances in the first period. The first was a shot from 25 yards by Billy Bonds that Pat Jennings fumbled uncharacteristically, before recovering to paw it round the post. The other was a Ray Stewart header from a Devonshire corner that came back off the bar with Pat Rice a spectator on the line.

The second half was a combative midfield affair with Brady and Sunderland and Devonshire and Brooking fighting for supremacy and chances few and far between.

As the game was heading towards extra time, Hammers made a break down the left, and Brooking slipped a neat pass through to seventeen year old Paul Allen, the youngest ever player in an FA Cup Final, who sidestepped Graham Rix's challenge, accelerating down on goal with real pace. He pulled away from the last defender, Willie Young, avoiding his clumsy and lunging tackle, and rounded Jennings to coolly slot the ball home.

Ecstasy!

The stadium erupted with a noise that belied the pre-match press suggestion that West Ham would only have 30,000 fans at the final. Allen's joy was as extreme as his emotional goal celebration, running to the half-way line to hug manager John Lyall. Lyall had decided to play him despite the more senior squad options at his disposal, and the gamble had paid off.

Arsenal tried everything they could in those last two minutes to pull themselves back into the game, but West Ham's defence held firm, especially Ray Stewart and captain Billy Bonds, the latter of whom was named man of the match soon after the game. It was Bonds' first career trophy, and after the long climb of the Wembley Stadium stairs and in the white West Ham change strip, he lifted it to high acclaim from the Hammers' fans. Gary and I stayed around at the ground with thousands of other fans for nearly an hour after the game had finished, joining in the celebrations and the general intoxicated mood of indefatigability felt by all supporters of the team that were once again the pride of London.

The reality of the developing issues in my life crystallised some days after the Hammers' Wembley victory. I knew that I would have to let Vivien know that things would soon be changing, that Chloe had come back into my life, and it wasn't fair on either of us to prolong something that I now knew had no future. My mind switched effortlessly to accommodate the new belief. All I had to do now was tell her …

Chapter Eight

The Shape of Pears to Come

So much for a new decade. The year is almost over and I am struggling to think of anything positive to come out of it, so far.

Starting on the highs, at least there's Geoffrey – as I'm now calling him. I think 'Geoff' sounds a bit harsh for an eight month old kid. Names get broken down into single syllables once a child has begun to establish their identity. Even from the most over-enthusiastic parenting perspective I can't yet see a personality in Geoffrey. He laughs, cries, eats and shits with the same degree of rounded expertise, but I've held back on asking him for his thoughts on the Iran-Iraq war. He could surprise me, and his first word (which we're still waiting for) could be 'abrogate', but I'm not holding my breath.

It's been an unmitigated mess on the home front. Vivien and Geoffrey are living in the flat in Clapham, but it's not the kind of place a kid should grow up in. A kid should have a garden. Somewhere to run around in safety. Clapham Common is surrounded by the South Circular, with juggernauts and police cars whacking round every corner at breakneck speed. Sometimes even I wonder whether I might end my life as an flattened imprint on the tarmac looking up at the underbelly of some articulated lorry.

We're still working it out. Vivien's mum has decided that she's not coming round to the flat 'at any price', which is actually a relief, as I was about to ban her. I had been hoping, in a new era of world tolerance, that I might have a personal crack at defeating the world's worst clichés, starting with the crap mother-in-law, only to fall at the first girdle.

We've stopped talking about who might be the father. There should be a few clues offered in the years to come, but even Vivien has realised that both of us have to follow through on our responsibilities to the boy. At least money issues are limited at the moment. You can handle almost anything if you've got money and an ounce of common sense.

So long as you're not John Lennon. Whilst I've never been the world's greatest Beatles' fan, Lennon getting shot in New York last week, apparently in front of his own home by some lunatic autograph hunter, made me feel suddenly mortal. If his driver hadn't grabbed the gunman from behind when he realised what was happening, Lennon might even have been killed. The driver had accompanied them to the front of the building because he'd forgotten the pass to operate the car park entry gate. Turns out the gunman was some kind of crazed fan, with a novel take on how to thank his hero for signing his book. Bet Lennon's really glad he decided to make his new home in New York City. Americans and guns. Not a great combination.

GB has taken up his first management position. He's gone to Wimbledon FC, newly promoted to the Football League in the late seventies, who, after a surprise promotion to the Third Division, had been relegated back to the Fourth, and were odds on to go straight out of the league again. It was the sort of football bet that my dad would say he had put £20 on, 'at excellent odds of 20-1,' only to forget he had ever said it when the prediction came true.

'So where's the £400 quid, dad?'

'Don't be ridiculous, son. Where would I get £20 from?' And so on.

I won't be putting any of my hard earned against GB's chances of keeping them up. I've followed his illustrious training career into management and I reckon he might surprise a few people. He's not short of confidence, and if he can communicate that fact to his players, 'little Wimbledon' could turn some heads in the next few seasons.

Things aren't quite so good at Palace, though. Kenny Sansom has, rather predictably, gone to a 'bigger club' – Arsenal – and Palace have accepted two players plus payment in return. A nineteen year old Clive Allen and a reserve keeper Paul Barron came to Selhurst Park as part of the deal. Just when Palace were beginning to look like they wanted to stay in the First Division, the management decide they want to cash in. Venables had already let us know that things weren't going too well with him and 'the suits upstairs' (a slightly inaccurate phrase considering none of them wore suits, and the Palace Board hadn't actually held an official meeting at the ground since 1973) and a day of reckoning was 'in the offing'. The day came in late October, and Venables was off to Queens Park Rangers. The club's stunning myopia in allowing such a promising young manager to leave as a result of their lack of ambition, was only compounded by the breathtaking news that – and this takes some believing – the Cuban Carbunkle might be the man to get us out of a hole. *That they had just dug themselves.*

Palace are currently being caretaker managed by Ernie Walley, a popular long-serving member of the coaching staff, of whom most of the players are also rather fond. We certainly think that he is a better long term bet than the furniture porn king. Whether what is left of the squad (John Burridge, Mike Flanagan and Terry Fenwick have all gone to Rangers to join Venables in the last few weeks) has any clout with the Board, we shall see. History would suggest that the thought of Bloye or anyone else on the Board soiling their shoes in the changing-room to ask our opinion about anything is nothing short of fantasy. So do I care? I have the best part of two years left on my contract. But it isn't just the money. I would rather be playing in the First Division than be in a team freefalling down towards the Third – a journey that carries with it reminders of our last great descent under the God of Drop (Terry Venables had once referred to Allison as 'The Great Relegator').

It was actually the hardest thing I had ever had to do in my life. I hadn't even told Chloe that I was seeing someone else. Or to be more accurate, had been in a relationship with that someone else for almost a year. There didn't seem to be any need. Chloe and I were drifting gently back into a relationship ourselves, and had been meeting once a week, usually ending up at her place more than mine. Her flat was nearer most of the places we went out to, and her mate Jenny had just been given a six month contract with an American fashion company so she'd be roaming the States for a living. I didn't need to crawl around on my hands and knees sniffing around for forgotten condoms or the secreted evidence of another female. Would Chloe have even cared? Not at that stage perhaps. But it didn't matter anyway. Vivien and I were a misplaced item, soon to be returned.

Or so I thought. I had been right at first in my feeling that this might not be as easy as simply closing a door on a fading part of my life. I hadn't seen Vivien for nearly three weeks, partly because I'd been focusing more on Chloe and partly because she'd been working nearly full time in her mum's grocery shop on the Harrow Road. Even before I'd married her daughter, mum and I hadn't seen eye to eye, so we'd made a point of staying out of each other's way.

The difficulty was that I had to actually arrange to see Vivien – almost make a date of it – somehow re-emphasising our relationship rather than doing something that might have begun to let her down gently.

There was nothing gentle about the evening.

I had agreed to go to the cinema, something we very rarely did, but which she had made a big deal about for that very reason. Quite why I might accede to her request when the whole point of the evening was to put an end to things, wasn't very clear. Not then, and still less now. Vivien wanted to go and see *The Elephant Man*. Her Spanish friend Rosita had said that she should see it, that it was 'a brilliant film'.

I didn't know David Lynch then, and hadn't heard of the film. I thought from the title that it might actually be a comedy, and that we might be able to call it a day with a laugh afterwards, rather than entrenched in the misery of some pseudo-drama of our own.

Twenty minutes into the film, and there's this John Hurt line about 'I am not an animal – I am a human being ...' She cried all the way through it. Not one of my better decisions.

'Just because one of your poncey football mates decides he should be going out with a model, you don't have to.'

'I don't want to go out with a model,' I lied. 'It's just that it isn't really fair on you. You're always saying how you want to be independent, and ...'

'I am independent!'

'There you are,' I said. 'And you can be more independent without me.'

'I don't want to be without you,' she said, somewhat paradoxically.

'We're under pressure,' I began, wondering just why I had decided to make an alter ego out of myself.

'You're under pressure?'

'It's difficult for footballers to remain in a committed relationship with everything that goes on in our lives. I'm only 26 for God's sake! We're not living in the nineteenth century!'

'You're a fake, Roy. Admit it. You don't believe what you're saying any more than I do. Go on, then, if you want to go off with someone else. There's little point me trying to stop you. I just hope she's worth it.' This last comment as she crossed the corner of Lonsdale Road and Portobello. It had started to rain heavily, and I was the only one who had an umbrella. For a moment I wanted to run after her. She looked sexy in the rain, holding the paper over her head to keep her dry, her flowered skirt clinging to her legs as she hurried away.

Why couldn't there be two of me to carry on both relationships in uncomplicated comfort?

She had handled the moment much better than me, and she hadn't even known it was coming. Maybe that was the point. She was the only one of us being honest. She was the only one being a real person. She had called me a fake! She was right.

I've realised I can't possibly play under Malcolm Allison again. I can't. Something about him reminds me about my dad. Or is it me I'm reminded of? Not the flamboyance, not the confidence, not even the ability to inspire others (yes, he has that, I have to admit − look at Charlie …). It's the belief that he is absolutely right. That no-one should question his judgement or his ideas or even his way of life. Despite the evidence everywhere that he is more often wrong than not, we are all supposed to accept him, to understand him, to tolerate him.

While I was at Manchester City, I'd begun to look more closely at what might be making him tick. He'd given me a fantastic deal to leave Palace and come to Maine Road, really made it worth my while to take it up as a career move. In many ways, he had made it irresistible. I wouldn't, couldn't deny him. I was the kind of person, he must have surmised, and he may even have been right at the time, who would reward that kind of offer with loyalty. I had made the journey up there, taken his advice about where to live, what car to get. I even moved my bank to his bank up in town. Even Charlie had thought changing the branch was a stupid idea.

Allison had played on my overrated notion of loyalty. I had joined in the team banter about him, laughing at his clothes, his antics and the things he said on television about football, but I had recognised some-where in my beliefs about people, that he actually liked me. That he went out of his way for me. I was only an average player at Palace who'd been lucky. He'd made me more than that by having City put in such a bid for me that I was bound to be signed. Even after he was sacked, they were forced to up their selling price in order to buy me back. I owed this man a great deal, maybe even my career. This man I criticised mercilessly. I couldn't work under him again.

Winning the FA Cup had been as much a help as a hindrance to the Hammers. John Lyall was now on a hiding to bugger all for the 1980-81 season if he didn't take the team back into the First Division. It'd be the third time of asking, already two seasons too long for the impatience of the devoted Upton Park faithful. The problem was that West Ham would be competing in the European Cup-Winners Cup for the second time in their history. This could not be allowed to become a distraction for the team. A Return to the First had to remain the priority at all times.

Nothing in my success as a player had reduced my enthusiasm as a fan, and it was still hard to say which I preferred out of playing for Palace or watching West Ham. I didn't get many opportunities to get to Upton Park, but could often make a midweek or cup game when Palace had no commitments. The novelty value of my rare status as a fan on the terraces probably gave such outings the edge over actually playing.

Hammers finally eased their way to the top of the tree in October and apart from a three match blip, it's where they will stay throughout the season. With Palace bottom of the First Division by the end of October, and still there as Christmas approaches, it's looking as though Palace may drop out of the Big League just as West Ham enter it. There is a certain karma in all of this that I've yet to fathom, but it boils down to another chance missed to play at Upton Park in the top flight.

The European adventure is proving a distraction, though, and in ways that West Ham United could never have imagined. Palace's midweek fixture against their nemesis Brighton on 17th September had been moved to Boxing Day, so I could have gone to the first Cup-Winners Cup game, away to Spanish team Castilla. There were good reasons to go, not just because it was West Ham's first time in Europe for seven years, but because Castilla shared Real Madrid's Bernabeu Stadium, a monster of an edifice that promised a wonderful atmosphere whichever team's game it hosted.

Geoffrey had been unwell over the weekend, so I decided it made sense to stay home. I'd also been out looking at houses in the past month, as we needed more space now we were a family. The flat had always seemed more than ample for my needs, but once Vivien and a baby arrived, it was clear that we would all need a lot more space. Towards the end of the evening, the news bulletins were beginning to run with a story that made me realise my decision not to fly out had been the right one.

Football hooliganism as a concept had come out of embryo in the 1970s, despite dating back a great deal longer. As a fan I could still remember the regulation Levi sta-prest jeans, and the claret and light blue two-tone scarves tucked under the belt over the right thigh as neatly as a perfectly knotted tie. This was how the West Ham fans walked two by two up Green Street to the ground in the late sixties when I first started going to matches. The head of each fan would be groomed either to a number one or razored to the skin, so that the column of men must have looked from the sky like a conveyor belt of upright uncooked sausages.

On many occasions, especially after the games, the funereal column would suddenly disperse at speed and seeing those grave pious expressions on each running man's face always generated a tightening in my stomach. After a Manchester United game I had seen five West Ham fans kicking a cornered United fan in the stomach as he lay, prostrate on the ground, his hands weakly raised in defence. At the cry of two policemen, the violators had broken up, leaving the quietly sobbing man curled up in a small heap, still trying to ward off invisible kicks with a bloodied arm. I had stood around, horrified and yet fascinated at the blood. Why would anyone want to hurt someone that badly just because of the team he supported?

I had continued to wear my scarf in the cult fashion, but my hair was never cut that short again. I didn't want the possibility of being mistaken for one of those angry lunatics I saw on that Saturday.

Fashions changed, but the threat of perpetrated violence remained the same at football matches throughout the seventies. The police, it seemed, were powerless to stop rival gangs meeting up before and after games to kick twenty colours of shit out of each other. There even seemed to be some kind of hybrid honour amongst different sets of fans as they set up meeting places to do battle. Cleverly scheduled late arrangements for the venues meant that the police would usually be in the wrong place at the right time, only getting to the scene of the action once everything had finished.

The form of the team in question wasn't always a specific cause of the violence, but if the team was losing it might just tip the scales. On this Wednesday, late in September 1980, several of the West Ham United klans had got themselves over to the Bernabeu Stadium an hour before kick-off, ready to represent their team and country in whatever pre-match entertainment they could organise with the Spanish locals.

Despite what must have been obvious to the airline officials at Madrid airport or anyone who could tell the difference between an English and a Spanish number plate, no-one seemed prepared for what happened that evening. Something like eight hundred West Ham 'fans' got onto the terraces when the ground opened, and busied themselves in the consumption of several litres of beer, obligingly provided by the clueless ground staff, until the local fans arrived. There had been a few disturbances outside the ground a couple of hours before the match, but nothing compared with what was about to happen.

Fighting broke out on the terraces around thirty minutes before the kick-off, which was delayed as some of Spain's finest responded to the belated alarm call from those at the ground. The police weren't going to let the fact that Franco had been dead for five years get in the way of a good opportunity to beat the crap out of several hundred English hoodlums. Even the Spanish fans suggested that the police might have been a little heavy-handed on the night.

The game got underway thirty-five minutes late, and Castilla, a set of players employed as Real Madrid's reserve side, recovered from an early David 'Psycho' Cross goal, to run out 3-1 winners on the night, all their goals coming in the second half of the second half.

Following the game, worse was to happen as the fans broke up into small groups around the town, each looking for someone to take their disappointment out on. In the disturbances that followed, three West Ham fans lost their lives, and thirty-four local fans were taken to hospital with various injuries varying from a dislocated elbow to a broken jaw. One had his leg crushed by a coach attempting to escort fans swiftly from the scene.

The new Prime Minister Margaret Thatcher, voted in as predicted in May 1979, made a statement about the need to restore the reputation of Britain abroad after the 'lunatic few' had sullied its name. The tabloids went berserk the next day, dragging out the old classics 'Thugs', 'Animals' and 'Morons' and a couple of impressive new ones – 'Vermin' and 'LowLife'. All I could think of at the time, watching from the back room, was how relieved I was that Geoffrey had had the colic all week. Two hundred fans were kept in local prisons overnight, and FIFA declared that West Ham would have to play the second leg at least 300 kilometres from Upton Park. It seemed a strange punishment, but the Spanish team declared themselves satisfied with the decision. In the event, before plans to play at Newcastle United's St James' Park could be finalised, West Ham's appeal was heard, and they were told they would be able to play the second leg at Upton Park after all, but behind closed doors. The fact that there had been no Spanish fatalities may have accounted for the rather lenient punishment.

When the second leg came round at the beginning of October I got to see the game, as it was televised. The strange atmosphere where the echoing shouts of the players were heard competing with the sounds of the local traffic was captured perfectly by the television crew from ITV who were allowed to film the game that night. West Ham won the match by the same score, 3-1, and the tie went to extra time. The Spaniards' legs had tired, and if anything, the lack of atmosphere seemed to have worked more effectively against them, Hammers piling in another three goals, Paul Hegarty completing his first hat-trick for the Hammers, who were now through to the Second Round.

The general consensus in the press was that West Ham had got away lightly, and that it was time to show these football hooligans that they couldn't dictate how football was run through their loutish behaviour. Odd, because that was exactly what they had done. The team had suffered in the end, rather than the fans, few of whom were punished for their actions. Most of those kept overnight in Spain a fortnight back were freed without charge the next day, and allowed to go home. Questions were asked about the availability of alcohol, and it was the first time for a while that the idea of identity cards for travelling fans was mooted. The three dead West Ham fans turned out not to have been 'vermin' after all – they were just innocent travelling supporters who had got in the way of something more serious. After some debate, a small plaque with their names on was placed in the main entrance to the ground. When I finally got round to seeing it some years later, I was relieved to see that those at the club who had put it there had decided against embellishing it with a corny Latin phrase.

This was the first of many incidents involving football hooligans that were going to populate the 1980s and change the sport forever. If only we could have seen the warning signs then, we might have found some way of nullifying or diverting the developing cancer of violence.

After six months of looking, and almost giving up, I finally found the right house for us, somewhere that could offer the previously elusive qualities of seclusion and easy access to London. The only down side due to the cost of £55,000 was that I would have to honour the remainder of my contract at Palace, and I'd have to play consistently well to make sure I got offered another one. If not at Palace, maybe some-where different, possibly somewhere better.

The house was just behind Wimbledon Lawn Tennis Club, within walking distance of the village. It was found for me by Gary, who'd heard about it from one of the business investors in Wimbledon FC. Not only did I get it at a 'reasonable price' – as indicated by the crazy money it ordinarily took to buy a place round there – but all my money went straight into the club just a mile down the road in Plough Lane, into their tiny 5,000 capacity ground. If Wimbledon ever got into Europe, playing fixtures behind closed doors might not prove such a difference from ordinary league games.

The next few weeks were the best I'd had for some time, and it was-n't because of what was going on at Crystal Palace. Malcolm Allison was back at Selhurst Park, it has to be said a wiser man, but even in the few months he'd been back, he'd realised that he wasn't going to be able to save the club from relegation without the cash to buy new players. The only cash the Board had released to him was whatever he had been offered in his one year contract – we never did find out what that was, and nor did the press, who were camped out at the ground almost every day, awaiting some new piece of scandal or intrigue that might set their slow moving March news train back into life again.

West Ham United were looking at the possibility of beating Middlesbrough's record points total to win the Second Division. Winning it wasn't in any doubt – their nearest rivals, the unfashionable Notts County and Swansea City, a good twelve points behind them. They had also managed to progress to the semi-finals of the European Cup-Winners Cup, where they were to meet Feyenoord of Holland over two legs for the right to play FC Jena (East Germany) or Benfica (Portugal) in the final at the Rheinstadion in Dusseldorf. This was a final I was determined to go to if they got there and I was able to get a ticket, hooligans or no hooligans.

Geoffrey was One Year Old, and to celebrate his birthday we had his new room done out in light claret and blue pastel colours with a World Cup football poster of the England team from 1966 and of West Ham's championship side from 1973. This was before we had even had the new kitchen installed, but then – I found myself chanting the mantra that was part of the new house – 'the kid comes first'.

It seemed remarkable that I had thought I might turn away from this little thing in my life, this wet, defecating, screaming, giggling ball of love. It wasn't his fault, and I would never make it his fault, even in the very darkest days to come. I continued to cling to the most likely naive notion that everything happens for a reason, whether it was football or 'real life'. Working hard at analysing just why certain things happened was the only challenge this philosophy presented.

Looking at the Football League tables in the penultimate week of the season brought Charlie back into my thoughts. He had been substitute for the Palace v Manchester City fixture at Selhurst Park back in March, and had stayed over at the flat (which I'd kept on) for the Sunday after the game in order to look up a few old friends. I had given him the keys, but as I'd had to get back home after the game and hadn't been up for clubbing, we'd hardly spoken.

When I'd picked the keys up from a neighbour and gone back into the flat, anticipating God knows what, I'd been amazed. There were two newly emptied whisky bottles, almost the only indication that he had even been there, other than a couple of clogged ashtrays and a hurriedly made bed. Not even a note. I'd stood at the lounge window of the flat looking out across Clapham Common, wondering about our friendship.

We'd both grown up together, known each other all our lives, and were now heading towards the end of our twenties. Crystal Palace had lost the game 1-0 to a freak goal from City's new £1 million pound signing from Nottingham Forest, Trevor Francis, who'd sliced a cross over the Palace keeper. The newspapers had all thought he'd meant it, but he hadn't. The manager, John Bond, yet another ex-West Ham player from that side of the late fifties, was about to substitute Francis, but the goal changed his mind. Consequently, Charlie and I didn't meet on the pitch. When I went to the players' bar after the game, he'd gone.

A couple of London sides had made bids for him that season, but he wasn't prepared to make the drop that any move would have necessitated. Was that part of how he had changed? Was 27 too old for a footballer to face a new challenge? The life seemed to have been squeezed out of him, this man who had more talent under his toenails than I had in my whole body. I'd imagined we were sharing something in our football careers, but perhaps it was all some kind of abstract coincidence. He had been vital in helping me join Palace, he'd given me encouragement and made me see football for what it was. He'd used his influence to get me transferred to Manchester City, a good experience for me. Going back to Palace had been my decision. The first move I had made in my career without him. Since then we had seen very little of each other.

Before I left the flat I noticed something I'd missed when I'd first come in. He'd left a sheet of paper by the phone. It was an alphabetical list of all the London sides, and 'Arsenal' had been punctuated with an exclamation mark. I hadn't had to look at him for too long on that substitute's bench to know that he wasn't happy at City. Maybe he had a plan after all.

West Ham didn't make it in Europe. The Feyenoord of 1981 were just too strong for them, finally ready to come out of the shadow of their great Dutch rivals, Ajax. Although Hammers had overcome a very talented Dynamo Tbilisi side in the Quarter-Finals, Feyenoord won 1-0 in the first leg of the semi-final in Rotterdam, and despite West Ham winning 2-1 in a thriller at Upton Park, the away goal was enough to take them through to the final, where they beat Benfica 1-0 to win the trophy. West Ham's run in the Cup-Winners Cup that year had been more of a challenge than the competition that they had won in 1965. My disappointment was because I genuinely believe they were good enough that season to go on and beat the Portuguese team in the final.

			F-A
ECWC R1 L1	17th Sept 1980	Castilla (Spain) (a)	1-3
ECWC R1 L2	1st Oct 1980	Castilla (Spain) (h)	(aet)6-1
ECWC R2 L1	22nd Oct 1980	Timisoara (Rom) (h)	4-0
ECWC R2 L2	5th Nov 1980	Timisoara (Rom) (a)	0-1
ECWC QF L1	4th March 1981	Dyn Tbilisi (Rus) (h)	1-0
ECWC QF L2	18th March 1981	Dyn Tbilisi (Rus) (a)	1-0
ECWC SF L1	1st April 1981	Feyenoord (Hol) (a)	0-1
ECWC SF L2	15th April 1981	Feyenoord (Hol) (h)	2-1

Even as a Second Division side, John Lyall's team had proved they were good enough to muck in with the very best in Europe, and with Billy Bonds a new force in midfield, they were ready to make their mark in the First Division. They rounded off the season in style, securing the Second Division Championship record total of 66 points with a 1-0 away win at Sheffield Wednesday, thanks to Paul Hegarty's goal, which took him to a record 36 goals for the season, the most any West Ham United player had notched since Geoff Hurst's 40 in 1965-66.

		P	W	D	L	F	A	Pts
1	West Ham	42	28	10	4	85	29	66
2	Notts Co	42	18	17	7	50	38	53
3	Swansea	42	18	14	10	66	45	50
4	Blackburn	42	16	18	8	50	30	50
5	Cardiff	42	19	10	13	67	53	48
6	Leyton O	42	18	10	14	56	38	46

And what of Geoff Hurst in 1981? Gary was the one on the FA circuit, and always good for information to satisfy my incessant 'Where are they now?' quest. This was to date one of my least expected responses. There had been some hint that Hurst would go into management or scouting for a top club. It was rare even for those who had spent most of their careers in football's elite divisions to go straight into management at the top end. If you were an ex-footballer looking for employment with one of the top sides, you had to take the youth team or take on a part-time job, like a club scout. With a foot in the door, you might work your way through the ranks, as John Lyall had at West Ham United. No-one got straight in from nowhere, and this, it appeared, was the fate of Geoff Hurst.

My last mental picture of Hurst was of a man having a torch shone in his face, whilst trying to avoid falling down the narrow stone steps that led towards the exit at a West Ham United ground plunged into three day week darkness. He was squinting, and clutching at the intermittent strips of handrail that peppered the wall on his right. It wasn't the image of a World Cup Winner, so when I heard that he was now a double glazing salesman in Colchester, I wasn't quite as surprised as Gary had expected. You had to make ends meet, whoever you were, and Hurst was obviously no different.

Despite the predictable fall from grace, I found I had lost none of my sympathy for the man's plight, and wondered just how he was getting through the days in his new job. It would be impossible for him not to feel that there was something hideously unfair about all of this. Jimmy Greaves, Hurst's vocational nemesis, had just been appointed European FIFA representative, just four years after retiring from the game.

This 'job' and the salary it offered, at a figure not unadjacent to £40,000 a year, required attendance at a few press calls a month and the odd Board Meeting in Europe, to which he would be flown first class. He advertised shaving products and shirts as well as writing an occasional column for the *Daily Telegraph*. Hurst, in the meantime, was selling double glazing.

Another season over. West Ham are celebrating promotion whilst Palace are contemplating part whatever-it-is of their *Return to the Second Division* drama, featuring guest star Malcolm 'The Smoke' Allison. He probably won't be staying on for next season, so we've been told. The Board will spend the summer considering the future of the club. The only questions are likely to be how far should we fall and how fast? It does make you wonder how the fans can keep turning up at the ground, week in, week out, knowing what they must know now after all this time. Perhaps optimism is the national sport, not football.

I've been up in town for a quick drink with GB and a couple of the lads from the team. Palace ended their relegation season with a creditable 1-1 draw against Coventry City at home, and a rare goal for me, even though it was just a toe poke in at the far post from Tommy Langley's cross.

Now my heart is beginning to beat just slightly faster as I step out of the car, which I've parked round the corner to the club. I've just dropped Gary home, but I'm up in town now. The traffic has been surprisingly light this evening. There's an Italian restaurant that I still frequent for the odd lunch, usually in the week. But this is different. I can already see her at our table across the room crowded with waiters and the usual Saturday night suited crowd. She hasn't seen me yet, and the way she's sitting gives me another minute before she does. The roll of blonde hair catches the light, glistening, and I imagine her face.

I breathe in slowly, savouring the pre-moment. The nature of her job, my job, our limited time together; all of it means this is still possible.

CHAPTER NINE

Newly Romantic

It's a strange decision by the West Ham Board. This is a man who was thrown out of Old Trafford three months ago. He was sacked four days after Manchester United's 2-0 home defeat at the hands of Harry Redknapp's Bournemouth in the Third Round of the FA Cup. He's been on the television in the intervening months, and is clearly still high profile, but it was thought that he would never get another job in football management after the tirade following his sacking. But he has, and guess who's given him it? Yes, Ron Atkinson, as of Thursday April 18th 1985, is the new manager of West Ham United.

The Sun's headline 'It's Ron!' is one of several tabloid celebrations of one of the great popular football heroes. *The Mirror* prefers 'East End Ron', while the *Daily Star* has chosen the simpler 'Ron's back!', which is, after all, why they are all running the story in the first place. This is the first time West Ham have gone for an 'outsider' managerial appointment since Ron Greenwood in 1961, and certainly a first in terms of hiring a loudmouth. Every other West Ham manager to date has had the same placid disposition, the same focus on the job in hand, each refusing to be seduced by the appeal of a good flirt with the media. Now they have decided to put someone in charge of the team for whom the term 'controversial' might have been invented. It's difficult to imagine who seems the more desperate, West Ham or 'Big Ron' as he has become 'affectionately' known? Affectionate?

All of this has come about in the managerless months since John Lyall left West Ham to join Ron Greenwood in charge of the England team. With just over a year to go until the 1986 World Cup, Greenwood's success as England coach has convinced a success-starved

English public that this might be the tournament. Twenty years on from when England last won it, World Cup Glory is being talked of again. After Don Revie and Joe Mercer's failures in charge, Greenwood's 1983 appointment was broadly welcomed. Norwich City had won the FA Cup in 1982 following a second place finish in the Football League the season before, and additional good showings in Europe had convinced the FA that Greenwood was the man to bring pride back to the three lions badge. England had not qualified for a World Cup competition since 1974, having missed out in 1978 and 1982, and all that money, all that talent – and all that planning – maybe next year would be the year. Greenwood was now 63 years old, and not quite so sprightly on the training ground, so the man he was grooming to follow in his footsteps at West Ham – before they sacked him – had been asked to do the running around.

John Lyall had taken West Ham United back to the First Division with a record points finish after winning the FA Cup, and his Hammers team had enjoyed four seasons in the top ten since, their best effort a third position finish in 1983-84. Lyall was still only 44, and seen as the final part of the England jigsaw to guarantee success in the world's greatest football tournament. As a West Ham fan, it was like widening your closest sympathies to the support of the national side. This was the 'dream team' that West Ham had never actually seen. How would they have performed together as Ron and John at Upton Park? We'll never know, but I felt they might just be the right combination for England. We shall see.

Meanwhile 'The Other Ron' is coming to Upton Park. I'll have to call him that until I see how he does.

My so-called career has waned with the fate of the clubs I've been with. True to form, Allison left Palace in February 1982, less than a year after returning, with the club hovering at the bottom of the Second Division. Subsequent experiments with Dario Gradi and Steve Kember as managers proved to be just that, but we somehow rallied at the end of the season to stay up by the foreskin of our teeth.

The fans and the Board at Palace have become people divided by a common enemy, football nous. Ron Noades, a property developer lost in a football world, had found himself at the helm of a ship without a rudder in a stormy season. If it had been the case of organising a survey and closing a deal on a portfolio of properties in London, Crystal Palace FC would have been laughing. Noades, or 'Nodules' as he has been unfairly labelled by the fans, was determined to make his business acumen function for him as their saviour, and he promptly issued a promise to them that he would 'turn the club around within a year'. It was a statement somewhat undermined by the appointment of Alan Mullery as the new manager. This was akin to putting Margaret Thatcher in charge of the Miners Union. Mullery had enjoyed success as an excellent Tottenham and England midfielder, particularly in the 1970 World Cup, but once he'd hung up his boots, 'enjoyment' wasn't quite the term to describe any success he might have been aiming for in the world of football management. Whenever things went well, Mullery's mouth tended to get in the way. It had already led to him becoming the first England player to be sent off, in 1968, after arguments and retaliation in a European Nations Cup game against Yugoslavia. Then, as a manager with Brighton, doing unfeasibly well in the First Division, he fell out with the chairman and left the club. Mullery had, it's true, managed Brighton to successive promotions, but then he went to Charlton, under Noades, into a short period of sustained Second Division mediocrity. Despite the fact that he was on a three year contract at the Valley, Noades persuaded him to follow his route to Selhurst Park and 'do a job for him' there. There can't be many people who aren't aware that Brighton and Hove Albion, who let's remind ourselves Mullery managed for two years, are the absolute nemesis of Crystal Palace Football Club. And Noades brought this man with him to 'do a job' at Selhurst Park.

He certainly 'did a job'.

Suicide jockey.

My sister Debbie is eighteen. It doesn't matter that I have a son who is five. I have a sister who is eighteen. Debbie and I were close when I was living at home. I was overly-protective, I suppose you might say. After dad died, I was worried that she might become somehow damaged by the experience. She was old enough to be told what had happened, but not old enough to understand. A family *Catch-22*.

As a quiet girl, it was always a puzzle to work out just what she really thought of anything that happened in our subdued family existence, especially once dad had gone. There were the eighteen months he was 'away', which I used to try to give her a mature perspective on the situation. Then just when I felt she was beginning to deal with his departure, he made a permanent exit. We hadn't seen much of him in those months. His guilt, mum's silent anger, a healing interregnum. We hadn't filled the gap his first departure had left; how were we supposed to fill the second one?

She often said things that, at the time, seemed at the best precocious and at the worst – well, weird. About a year after dad left, mum started to make the effort to find someone. It was quite difficult, even for her twenty-three year old son, to watch it happening, and it must have had some kind of effect on her ten year old daughter.

'She's started going out a lot, and she doesn't tell me where. I don't want to get pushy, but I'm worried, Roy. She's a woman now, I know that, but then there's things you hear about. I don't want to spend the rest of my life worrying that I didn't say anything when I should have.'

I was spending a rare day at mum's, a few weeks before the new season started, at the house in Hendon we'd grown up in. She hadn't moved, even after the problems with dad. I'd offered to help her buy a place somewhere further out, but she preferred to stay put.

We were watching 'Live Aid', a cornucopia of musical talent brought together by Bob Geldof and Midge Ure on 13th July 1985 to raise money for starving children in Africa. Chloe had been ahead of her time with her ideas a few years back about mobilising the cash and efforts of the rich and famous to do something about the issues of poverty in the world. Simultaneously in Philadelphia and at Wembley, pretty much every well-known band you could think of was playing a short twenty minute set sometime in the day. Status Quo had opened the Wembley lunchtime section with 'Rocking All Over the World' and just an hour, after The Cure and Paul Weller, Joy Division were on stage singing 'Love Will Tear Us Apart', Ian Curtis joined on vocals by Siouxsie Sue.

I had spent some serious money on a giant colour television for mum, which had been installed with a stereo speaker system. The Live Aid event was broadcast simultaneously on television and in stereo on the radio, so with a tweak here and there, we were able to listen to a live concert in the front room, in fantastic stereo sound. I was even able to tape it in stereo on a video machine I'd bought the previous year. I could edit out the crap as we watched (which was about 75 per cent of it) and take the tape home to watch later. The tape quality on playback was almost as good as watching it live. These machines had cost thousands of pounds twenty years ago, but I'd bought mine for just £600!

Even with it being a charity event, there had still been a little bit of backstage bitching about who should appear as the main act. Queen and David Bowie had looked the best bet until Geldof had pulled off a stunning coup, and Paul McCartney had agreed to finish with a short acoustic set, accompanied by – John Lennon. It was well known that the two had met up in 1983 and put to bed most of their differences, but no-one had ever thought they would play live together again. Could this be the beginning of the Beatles reforming? Let's hope not. They were going stale with that last album. They should, as its title clearly suggests, 'Let it Be'.

'You're a bit quiet, Roy. What are you thinking about?'

'I was just thinking. What you said about Debbie is right, mum. I'm worried, too. I know I haven't see her much lately, but last time we were both here, I didn't feel I knew her. She's not up for babysitting, either. She used to come down to the house twice a week. Even stayed over now and then. I've stopped asking her since last April. Always too busy.'

'Well, there are boys on the scene …'

'And what about you?'

My mother just smiled. There wasn't quite the air of resignation in her expression that she had been showing over the last few years. She was fifty, but she was as sharp as a bread knife, and if she wanted something, she could usually get it. Stealth was her great talent, and she had it in abundance. She'd known about what dad had been up to well before he left, but she'd not issued ultimatums or the bag of histrionics that many women in the same situation might have done. She'd waited for him to come to his senses. But he never had. Now she'd come to hers and was getting on with her life.

Debbie, however, had been in work for a year, and was now going to St Martins Art College. Perhaps the whole bohemian thing might be right for her. It wouldn't have been as easy if dad had been at home. They'd have argued. They argued when she was seven. A few years would have stepped up the stakes. She didn't need anyone to fight her battles. The truth was that she didn't have any battles, so far as I could see. She did what she liked, and compared to some, she was still level-headed. Even if she did like Joy Division and The Fall.

'Big Ron' completed his month as West Ham's new manager, and his nine match record wasn't too bad. The fact that he had to play those nine matches in just thirty days was because of a vicious winter that had cauterised the whole of the January fixtures after New Year's Day. West Ham ended the 1984-85 season in twelfth position in the First Division, probably four or five places below what they might have achieved under John Lyall.

The squad that Atkinson inherited was already quite different from the one that Lyall had put together, but the talented nucleus suggested that any improvements he made were bound to lead to more silverware for West Ham. Lyall had left at the end of February, and within three weeks Paul Hegarty and Tony Gale had asked for a transfer. Neither played again for West Ham and were sold on to Celtic and Chelsea respectively at the end of the season.

Atkinson's First XI (1984-85): Les Sealey, Ray Stewart, Mark Dennis, Billy Bonds, Alvin Martin, Keith McPherson, Alan Dickens, Bobby Barnes, George Parris, Tony Cottee, Geoff Pike. Substitute: Alan Dickens

			F-A
20th April	Sunderland (a)	W	1-0
27th April	Luton (h)	D	0-0
4th May	West Brom (a)	L	1-2
6th May	Coventry (h)	W	1-0
8th May	Everton (a)	L	0-3
11th May	Sheff Wed (a)	L	1-2
14th May	Watford (h)	W	4-1
17th May	Ipswich (a)	W	1-0
20th May	Liverpool (h)	L	0-1

West Ham's form under Ron Atkinson, 1984-85: P 9, W 4, D 1, L 4, F 9, A 9, Pts 13

Tony Cottee, Alan Dickens and Alvin Martin were three of Lyall's finest products from the West Ham United Youth Academy, and for the time being, were staying put under the new Atkinson regime. If the Board were ready for a clearout, those three would certainly put plenty of money in the West Ham bank. Even West Ham's loyal fanbase might twitch numerically were any of them to depart.

'Big Ron' had added Keith McPherson and England Under-21 international Steve MacKenzie (from West Bromwich Albion) to his inherited squad, and taken some steps to putting a touch of his own style into the club. He was as prolific as ever on television, coining idiosyncratic phrases and tactical claptrap with every appearance. Whether he had a coaching ghost writer or had been secretly studying the semiology of sport, there was no-one quite like him in English football in 1985.

The house in Wimbledon had eventually been finished. The back room upstairs was the last one to be stripped of the miserable flowered wallpaper its previous inhabitant had used to torture unwelcome guests with. There was little joy in rounding off the last of the many decorating jobs that had faced me when I'd bought it. All that could happen now was that I would have to start focusing on what was inside.

A footballer's life hasn't changed much in the last 30 years. There's always time in the week when you're not training, and unless you're Jimmy Greaves, forever off on another media or advertising trail, that gives you time to reflect. In Manchester there had never been enough time to get round to the hundreds of women I wanted to sleep with. Charlie and I had organised five between us on one memorable evening. After that you start to realise that the appeal of a mountain of flesh is just another example of gluttony blinding the perpetrator. Ideas can be such mammoth entities. The reality often becomes just another 'one of many'.

I had spent a lot more time with GB, and would often train with Wimbledon when the Palace players were given a day off. It was a combination of wanting to keep myself fit – it always seemed harder to keep up now unless I was doing more. Training had never come naturally to me; it was more like a penance. That was all I think I liked about it. The feeling of pushing yourself into the beyond. I had been lucky enough to become a professional footballer, now I needed to be more than that.

I often felt I should have been something else; that becoming a footballer was just one grand accident. Things had fallen into place so fortuitously for me. I had always accepted them, celebrated their arrival. Marrying Vivien had all the false appeal of much of what had happened in my life. Like catching a bus in the wrong district, you get on in the hope of ending back where you started. The bus would take you there, which was good because on your own you might never find your way back.

While mum had been watching Queen singing 'We Are The Champions' on Live Aid, I had felt the irresistible urge to grab a football and go out in the back yard to practise kick-ups. And because there was one under the stairs, I had done it. My old leather football. The pump from Debbie's school bicycle and an adaptor from the kitchen's miscellaneous drawer, and I was counting those numbers again. Just two weeks earlier I had been playing in a five-a-side tournament for Palace at Wembley Arena against a celebrity team that included George

Best. Knocking the ball around in the yard had more poignance. It was a man trying to beat his previous achievements as a child. There wasn't the same level of seriousness, but there was the understanding that such activities and how we relate to them can define us. I felt the smile riding my face as I passed one hundred, keeping the ball up, trying to remain in the same square yard of land.

After a while I realised that mum was watching from the back door. I kept going. One hundred and thirty-four, one hundred and thirty-five … Why was it easier now? It wasn't a religion any more for me, but it had been. It still was for millions of boys – and girls – up and down the country. Two hundred and twelve, two hundred and thirteen … The routine was like driving down a narrow but busy lane, facing a giant double decker bus coming in the opposite direction. One turn of the wheel, one wobble of the bicycle as the lorry behind you decided to overtake. Three hundred and two, three hundred and three. I suddenly hit a rhythm, and ten or eleven kick-ups after I had, I volleyed the ball high in the air over the fence. I stopped for a moment and laughed. Then, suddenly aware of the significance of that ball, my ball, I ran out of the back gate and onto the green around the house. Despite the fact that Live Aid was on, some kids were playing a game of football on the green, with their coats down as goals. My ball had shot over the fence and beyond where they were playing, coming to a stop just inside the front of a house in the next street. It had remained there, untouched. The football match they were playing held their attention beyond the appeal of an uninvited leather ball. I walked round silently and collected it, and although one head turned momentarily from the game, nobody noticed me.

I have been stopped in the street, especially in Croydon, and had as many as thirty people round me, asking for my autograph, wanting to talk about their great love, Crystal Palace, once they knew they were suddenly in the company of one of the men who comprised the team that called themselves that. These Hendon kids on a green on a hot July Saturday only cared about their football game.

'You were like that, Roy,' mum said. 'Your father and I used to watch over the fence as the older boys tripped you up and played tricks on you in the game. You never gave up. Always went back for more the next night.'

'Dad was never interested in me playing football. He didn't come to any of the First XI games at school. Not even when we got to the semi-finals of the National England Schools Cup.'

'He did watch you,' she said. 'He told me he thought you were good enough to make it as a footballer.'

'Why did he never tell me, then?'

'He wanted you to get there on your own. Without his help. He was afraid that you'd resent him being ambitious for you.' She squinted from the direct sun as she spoke.

'Did he ever apologise to you?'

'For what?'

'For what he did.'

We were now back in the kitchen, and I had lazily grabbed the bottle of whisky I had seen hiding between the tea and sugar jars and was pouring myself a generous measure.

'You shouldn't, Roy. You're driving back.'

'Well, did he?'

'He didn't have to,' she said, finally. 'He made a choice. He wasn't a bad person, you know. People don't choose to leave their families to hurt them. If someone is incomplete as a person, they should be honest to themselves about who they want to be. Not how they want to be seen. Nothing your father did was intended to hurt us. And I think I always knew that he was somehow ... unfulfilled.'

My relationship with Chloe had begun to dress itself up as something neither of us had ever intended it to be. The problem was precisely because of its low maintenance engine. It might be a couple of days between seeing each other; it could be three months. The flat was a *pied-à-terre* in the week. Chloe was the only other person who had the key. We would meet there. She always asked about Geoffrey. I usually had a photo of him in his Crystal Palace shirt, looking broody.

We tended to meet during the day. She was abroad and in the States a lot, and had even gone into partnership with a friend of hers, lending her name and image to some farty French perfume. It was all very crafted and lucrative, but invariably temporary. Not unlike us, in many ways.

'Big Ron' had his critics, but he made the kind of start to the 1985-86 season with West Ham that won him many new admirers. He had always been an advocator of black players in his time at West Bromwich Albion and, to a lesser extent, at Manchester United. In the first five games of the season, Atkinson played three black players in his West Ham side: George Parris, Bobby Barnes and Laurie Cunningham, the

141

last of whom he had managed to sign on loan from Real Madrid, where the twenty-nine year old midfielder had become disillusioned. The fact that he was prepared to come to West Ham showed the kind of esteem in which he held Atkinson.

Cunningham was an immediate hit with the fans, though his inclusion came at the expense of Geoff Pike. In those five games, of which West Ham won three and drew one, the three black players played so consistently well, that when the *Daily Express* reporter William Steven called them 'The Supremes' after the Diana Ross black girl group in the sixties, the name stuck.

The club's PA official began playing Diana Ross' 'I'm Coming Out' each time the Hammers ran out of the tunnel at Upton Park. It wasn't quite the Supremes, but you knew what he meant. So long as the team were winning, the fans would be happy. Although the name was a media invention, Atkinson was happy to run with it, and on several occasions referred to the players as 'The Supremes' in press conferences after the games. It might have been more appropriate for the long-suffering West Ham fans if they had played 'You Keep Me Hangin' On'.

Gary's success at Wimbledon over a short period had been remarkable. The team had a long history in the amateur Southern League, only to suddenly win promotion to the Fourth Division at the end of 1976-77. When GB took over, they were in the Fourth Division, but after four seasons of graft and some of the most stunning squad shuffling ever seen in the League, he had guided them to the Second Division at the end of 1983-84. The following season was the one I chose to occasionally train with them. Gary was still manager and coach, and doing pretty much everything on a day to day basis at Plough Lane. He would often do a half hour stint selling programmes outside the ground just after 1 o'clock. The limited fanbase all loved him – he was the man they saw as responsible for the club's success, though it seemed to me that it was just as much the efforts of the squad, some who could still play one week in the centre of defence and the next in a midfield holding role. He asked and they delivered.

The 1984-85 season became in effect a holding operation for Gary. The Dons finished twelfth, but they scored successes over some illustrious teams, and still had a chance of promotion up to the end of February when their form became sluggish and the wins dried up.

I'd been in football for thirteen seasons, and at the age of 31, my choice of options was narrowing. Crystal Palace had become a regular

Second Division side, too good to go down, but not enough talent or inspiration to go up. At least so long as 'Nodules' had anything to do with the running of the club. It got so mediocre that there were now people on the terraces who pined for the days of Malcolm Allison. Fame at any price, even if it had very little to do with football.

I had spent more and more time with GB as the season progressed, once it became obvious that his side wasn't going to get the Big Promotion. He had jokingly asked me to join him back in 1981 when he'd started there, but now it was both of us hovering towards the same suggestion. I desperately wanted to stay in the game once I'd stopped playing; I had seen so many bad managers in my time in football, but I had also seen the true greats: Greenwood, Cantwell, Lyall, Clough and Revie. Men with a history of success in their time in football, and all had been in their posts long enough to prove that their achievements were no fluke.

Since I'd met Gary, I'd realised that this was the kind of job I relished. Being in the position to motivate players; to get hold of a team by the scruff of the neck and get them to a position where winning could become a habit. And Gary had a team of winners, though how he had got them all together at the same time was anyone's guess. Beasant, Cork, Evans, Winterburn, Gage, Galliers, Fairweather. Names from nowhere, but a team who could beat anyone on their day. Whether it was the claustrophobia many teams complained about playing on the Plough Lane pitch, whether it was the sheer sensation that this team should simply not be in this division – it was never clear. They had proved that the Football League wasn't always simply about money; that the little teams could occasionally rule the roost.

I watched GB in action, on the training ground and at the matches. He definitely had something about him that was unique in football management. He was utterly unflappable, and had the patience to tame a class of unruly schoolkids. He had trained to be a teacher at one time – I often felt that might have been the key to his success.

We spent a few evenings mulling over things, and eventually decided that I would look at my contract and see if there was a way of swinging a departure with Palace, who were now managed by the 29 year old ex-England and Manchester United player Steve Coppell. Mullery had been sacked after three seasons of unadulterated kak, the first decision from 'Nodules' that had made any sense in all his time at Palace. When Coppell was invited to take the job, I had been initially suspicious that it was a cheap gamble of an appointment by Noades, but Coppell had steadied the ship and got the side playing with passion again.

I could see, however – usually from the dugout – that this was a team going places – without me. I was older than the manager, for God's sake, and the new blood promised great things for the future. John Salako, Andy Gray and Ian Wright were all young and hungry and fresh legs in from the youth team. My latest contract was up at the end of the season, and it didn't seem likely that it would be renewed. There was something different about Coppell, something professional, a man without bullshit.

In the first week of December, I went out for a meal with GB to our local Indian in the Village. Wimbledon had won three on the trot and were now at the top of the Second Division for the first time in their history, looking eyeball to eyeball at the possibility of a footballing future as a club in the top flight. Despite the tiny Plough Lane attendances, Gary had worked out that the share of the revenue generated from away games would still be enough to pay the wages of the players (his first concern) and keep the Football League's legal department off his doorstep (his other major worry).

He was the only manager in the Second Division who ruled from his office and from the training ground. He needed a coach, and I had seen enough of his methods over the last two seasons to know that it was a job that I could do. If there was ever a good time to join a team, it was with them top of the Second Division, seven places higher than Crystal Palace. It was an upwards move for me in every sense, not least in terms of geography, with the house almost walking distance to the ground.

The interview with Coppell went perfectly. He suggested we work out a reasonable fee and look at the possibility of going before the end of January. I had bargained on leaving at the end of the season, but wasn't going to argue. My career looked likely to have developed well for the future as a result of the move, and to be able to continue playing as well for the time being was an added bonus.

For all the delight of my career, football in England was in a mess. The regional luck-of-the-draw coverage of games from the seventies had developed into an all-out street fight between BBC and ITV with the gloves off for exclusive rights to games. ITV had already shown the first ever live game in the 1982-83 season, a 2-1 win for Tottenham over Nottingham Forest, but even then the public could see that this wasn't quite the same thing as seeing edited highlights on Saturday night or Sunday lunchtime.

I had never really been that bothered about watching football on television, probably because I was rarely on it. I would watch if Charlie had scored for City or if West Ham had enjoyed a good win, but as these were both rare events, I continued to prefer the company of people over a night in with the telly. The season after the first live games were transmitted, the unions started to get involved with the television companies over whether games were to be edited locally or nationally, and over the disproportionate amounts of money being offered to whoever did whatever. A blackout followed of all ITV football coverage in 1983, over ten years after the one that had prematurely curtailed my conversation with Geoff Hurst at Upton Park. This one, however, lasted five months.

Football is now suffering yet another TV blackout, timed to miss the beginning of Ron Atkinson's first full season at Upton Park. Can't be all that bad, then. Just more history that no-one will have any footage of. I might even have chosen to tape the football on my video machine if it was happening. But it isn't. This blackout is over the latest offer that ITV have made for exclusive rights to show live footage. The Football League want more. ITV won't give in.

In the end, just before Christmas, the Football League, starved of TV revenue, jack it in and go with the original ITV offer. So now we have live football again. All that fuss over nothing? Ronny 'Nodules' has told us that more TV money will mean higher wages for players. The kids at the club all think he's right, but I'm not so sure. More money for chairmen, perhaps.

With the media's new fascination with football, ITV have launched a new Saturday lunchtime show in place of the now defunct *World of Sport*. The idea of the show is to preview that afternoon's Football League programme and also to give their highlights programme a giant plug. They have been showing trailers for it all week, and I confess that I am already hooked before they've even showed the first episode. It's called *Saint and Hurstie*, and is fronted by two famous ex-footballers, Ian St John and Geoff Hurst. My first thoughts are that maybe Hurst should have stuck to selling double glazing, but then one of the trailers catches my eye. Hurst has been cast as the joker, it would seem, to Ian St John's Scottish straight man. The idea is that Hurst travels to the grounds and changing-rooms of different clubs all over the country to interview players and managers in a somewhat irreverent style. From my recollection of how 'straight' he was when I met him at Upton Park, I thought that the whole idea wouldn't have a chance of working. But it looks like 'Hurstie' might actually have carried it off.

It's not as though he hasn't had some experience in the media. Hurst was the summariser for Central TV a couple of years ago, and had established a banter routine with the commentator Gary Newbon. Central have a record over the years, however, for some fairly eccentric behaviour. After the West German President, in the UK on some European Community visit, said something about Hugh Johns' legendary 1966 World Cup commentary from the final, 'the war's finally over – the Germans will have to surrender now!' they promptly sacked him. That was ten years after he'd said it! So why shouldn't they hire Geoff Hurst, a man whose goals he might have been screaming about on another day?

'Hurstie' has a catch phrase that they're already touting on the trailers for Saturday's programme, 'You didn't mean to do that, did you?' It has already been used to describe a shot from Mark Hughes that hits Gary Bailey in the face, and a soup serving in the canteen at QPR from manager Jim Smith that misses the plate and drops on to the boots of defender Gary Waddock. I am too big a fan of Hurst to listen to the nagging voice in my head telling me it's going to be a disaster of Niagra Falls proportions. I'm already practising the catch-phrase for tomorrow's training at Holmesdale.

Under this worthy attempt to put a bit of humour back into football, lies the fact that no English clubs are competing in Europe in the 1985-86 season. This is after a FIFA ruling, condemning the behaviour of Liverpool fans on the 29th May at the Heisel stadium in Brussels at the European Cup Final where they ran riot in the ground before the game against Juventus, causing the deaths of 39. Incredibly, the game was then played, Juventus winning 1-0, but four days after, investigations were carried out and the sentence was issued. The actual pronouncement said that 'all English clubs' are 'banned indefinitely' from playing in Europe. It is inevitably a consequence of the significance of that game combining with the number of dead. I suddenly find myself remembering West Ham's game against Castilla back in September 1980, and wondering where the game of football is headed now in this country.

146

CHAPTER TEN

Missing You

I've found a condom in the bathroom waste bin. I rarely empty the bins round the house, but this morning Vivien has gone to the doctor's for a check-up, and the bin duty has fallen to me.

I hold it up experimentally to the light. It's fairly full, and at least the donor had the good manners to tightly tie the neck before condemning it to the waste bin. Despite my determination to treat Geoffrey as an adult as soon as is reasonably possible, it seems unlikely that this belongs to him. So whose is it?

Unfortunately, it isn't mine. I'm not averse to the things. These days they often feel like you haven't even got them on. However, someone has been getting it on in this house, unless the contents of that condom are mine, and if so, they'd have had to have been kept in a freezer for at least a year to be in the condition they're in.

Will she know I've found it? That's almost as significant as knowing the identity of the donor. My brain is skirting round the events of the past few days until I focus on the fact that I'm still holding the black bag into which I should be putting the rest of the bathroom waste.

Three minutes later and I'm downstairs, poring over a cup of tea in the kitchen. The flicker of anger I felt upstairs has subsided. She's a red-blooded woman with needs that I haven't been satisfying. Okay she's my wife, there's that, but I'm sometimes away from this place for up to three days at a time, travelling with the club or … elsewhere.

We've never talked about what one or the other might do on our days apart. There's an unspoken assumption that you don't behave like that, but it's more a secret wish than an assumption. Perhaps it's not surprising now that I'm thinking right back to when she told me about the men she'd slept with. I had had that picture of her running off in the rain, but what she told me that night had somehow stained the image.

'How could you have been so stupid?'

'It may sound stupid to you, but it made perfect sense to me. At the time.'

'But three different men in a week? Without protection?'

'I didn't need protecting. And are you telling me you weren't screwing everything that moved when you were up in Manchester? I have been with you, you know. So I know.'

She was lying on the couch in the flat, pissed. Pissed, but not to the extent that she didn't know what she was saying. And I'd asked her over. I wouldn't even have discovered half of this if I'd left her to it. Chloe had gone off to Paris for a fortnight, and my lower brain had got the better of me again.

Vivien had agreed to come round when I'd phoned her. We'd made out a couple of times, and in the throws of the second effort, the tears had started. Then the revelations.

'So what are we going to do?'

'We? You don't have to do anything. It's not your problem.'

'Oh I think it is.' We both looked down at the evidence before us.

'I see what you mean.'

I took a final swig of the tea as I heard the key turn in the lock.

'How did you get on?' I asked.

'Did you put the bins out?'

'Yes,' I said. 'So how did you get on?'

'Oh, I've got to go back next week. She gave me a blood test.'

I watched her as she came in. If she was acting, she was very good. If not, then there was the added insult that she could casually stuff a used condom into our bathroom bin without a thought for whether or not I might see it. A day later and it's forgotten. With Geoffrey gurgling in the next room. It was all getting a bit uncomfortable in my head. I was trying to keep away from the thought of who it might be.

'I'm taking the training today,' I said.

'Oh,' she said. 'I hope that goes okay.'

'Yeah.'

'I rang Debbie to babysit for Geoffrey because I'm out tonight.'

'She's not up for babysitting, so far as I know.'

'She's agreed to do it, so it's okay. I told her I didn't know if you'd be back.'

'I'm only going for a two mile drive down the A3 for God's sake. I'll be in. I can look after Geoffrey. I'll cancel Debbie.'

'Let her come round, Roy. She sounded like she was looking forward to it. You should spend some time with her. God, if my sister was as clued up as she is I'd have her round here all the time. Just a pity that she can't hold a job or a man down for more than a week.'

I watched her busy herself with the shopping she'd brought in. I couldn't bring myself to ask her where she was going. I wouldn't have ordinarily, so I couldn't do it now without raising suspicion that something wasn't right.

'Bye love,' she said, kissing me on the forehead like a dumb schoolboy. 'Back tomorrow afternoon.' The door closed behind her, and within a minute I could hear her Renault 5 automatic coughing into life in the distance.

Big Ron Atkinson is not working out at West Ham United. By that I mean the concept, not the man, although he does seem to have put on a few pounds in the last couple of months. His honeymoon period was rudely ended with transfer requests from Tony Cottee and Alan Devonshire. Devonshire's is the more surprising of the two, as he has only just recovered from the injury that kept him out of the team for the whole of last season.

No newspaper article has been able to satisfy my curiosity as to why the requests were submitted, though in the month since they were, the team hasn't won. This is a run of seven games that have yielded only four points, all from home draws. All three of the away games have been lost.

Perhaps Cottee and Devonshire are worried about their chances of playing for England in the World Cup in Mexico in June. Devonshire has to get back in the team, which he will if he hits form. Cottee, however, has only played a handful of international games, and is fifth choice striker at best. Greenwood and Lyall achieved their goal of qualification for the finals even before the last two home games against Turkey and Northern Ireland in October and November of last year. The only West Ham player permanently in the side is Alvin Martin, in the centre of defence. Cottee came on as sub against Romania last May in Bucharest in a game that ended goalless. He's still expecting Ron Greenwood (and John Lyall) to remember the 28 goals he scored in the

1983-84 season when West Ham finished third. All they'll remember is that they weren't scored in an England shirt.

I've been at Wimbledon FC for a fortnight. There's been a plateau period of three draws, but the club is still at the top of the Second Division. I'm feeling a slight suspicion from the players about my appointment. They know I've been a mate of GB's for some time, and most of them will have played against me in the Palace v Wimbledon games back in February and September 1985, but the fact that they are doing so well draws them inexorably to the old adage 'if it ain't broke, don't fix it'.

I've seen things in Gary's training that can be improved, and with a combination of ideas from Terry Venables and Steve Coppell and with a pinch of my own thoughts, my first training session gets underway. There are plenty of competitive activities, designed to keep the players hungry, even in training, and the 30 minute game is kept till the end to make the football activity the icing on the cake. I try to make everything seem a part of a focused goal; fitness, awareness and confidence.

It goes well, though I've already noticed my mind wandering when the team are all involved in activities. I need to resolve this little problem in my head so it doesn't start affecting my work.

Gary seems pleased with the way the training session went. Though I've told him that I'm happy to remain a squad player, he's now insisted on putting me in the starting line-up for Saturday as Wally Downes still hasn't recovered from the knock he got at Blackburn last week. I feel more nervous about that than I did about taking the training. It's all very well organising the instructions about how to play the game a certain way, but being out there and following through on my own rhetoric is a very different thing. Perhaps if I'd known I was going to be starting, I might have issued different instructions ...

Seeing Debbie that evening turns out to have been a good idea. She doesn't question why she's been asked to babysit when I'm at the house, and I get the chance to talk to her for the first time in ages. There are a few revelations in store for me that I realise I might have been avoiding hearing someone else make.

'You're lucky, you and Vivien leading the lives you do.'

'How do you mean lucky?'

'Well, mum and dad. You know. You two seem to be able to live your own lives and bring up Geoffrey. And you don't argue like mum and dad did.'

'Mum and dad never argued.'

'You know what I mean. That silent arguing. Sniping with comments. If I can remember it, you must be able to.'

'Not if they only did it in front of you. They probably thought subconsciously that you wouldn't understand. Wasn't that stupid of them.'

'You ever thought of – you know – having another one?'

'Another family? One's enough, thanks.'

'Someone for Geoffrey to play with. All my friends at college that are only children always talk about how they'd have enjoyed their lives more with a brother or sister.'

'One of the reasons that Vivien and I are lucky is that we only have one other person to worry about. Bringing up a child isn't easy, before you start getting broody.'

Debbie laughed. I could see no reason for mum to worry about her. She was bright, sensitive, and with mum's looks, hadn't any worries on that score either. She also seemed to see a little more around her than I did. So why would she make the comment about Vivien and I having this perfect relationship? Had that been a prompt for me to contradict her and start telling her … But she didn't actually say 'perfect relationship'. She talked about 'lucky lives', and that might not be too far from the truth. So why have I started worrying about Viv's old boyfriend Simon? The also possible father, making love to the possible mother of his possible son, definitely in the next room.

I suddenly know I am going to play a blinder on my debut for Wimbledon on Saturday.

Ron and the Supremes haven't had a hit for two months, and he looks edgy whenever cameras catch him at the training ground. There is a fantastic in-depth interview on *Saint and Hurstie* just before the Easter break, with the team third from bottom, that they've cryptically entitled 'Da Don't Run Ron'. I video the programme on the timer. Hurstie talks about playing for the Hammers in the sixties and draws Atkinson into making a few guarded comments about his management style. When he finally says that his players aren't hitting the target like they were at the beginning of the season, right on cue this ball flies out of nowhere and hits Big Ron smack in the face, knocking off his glasses and knocking him clean out of shot. After a short silence and some background laughter, presumably from the team filming it, Hurstie shouts out to the anonymous player who's smacked Big Ron in the face, 'You didn't mean to do that, did you?' The place falls about. Even Big Ron laughs. The only thing I can think is that he can't be that bad a bloke if he's given his permission to have that moment shown on national TV.

Whether it's the effect of Ron getting a smack in the face or not, West Ham lose all three of their games over the Easter break and find themselves bottom of the First Division. It's hard to think that this team was in Europe at the beginning of last season, even if they did go out in the first round. Big Ron's unlikely to be too worried about the indefinite ban on England teams in Europe, as he won't be going anywhere other than the dole office, the way the season is panning out.

	P	W	D	L	F	A	Pts
18 Leicester	37	8	11	18	59	75	35
19 Ipswich	37	8	11	18	51	71	35
20 Man City	37	9	7	21	29	50	34
21 WBA	37	9	5	23	27	70	32
22 West Ham	37	8	7	22	35	76	31

The last five games are all against teams in the lower half of the league except Nottingham Forest, who are eighth, so there are still chances of avoiding the drop. The fixtures that jump out are the penultimate one, away at West Brom, and the one before that at home to Ipswich. The only game I've been to all season at West Ham was a Milk Cup game (the Football League will take any sponsors, these days) home to Swansea City that Hammers won 1-0. Two weeks later they lost the away leg 2-0 and went out of the cup. That was Big Ron's first embarrassment of many in the Big Seat at the Boleyn. The odd thing is that West Ham still seem to be on television every other weekend now, as if the cameras are preparing to watch one of their own in the throes of death, like show biz vultures.

I have already worked out that West Ham are doomed. Wimbledon have won another three games (the first of these away to Sunderland, thanks to a last minute goal from yours truly) and are almost there. The unthinkable achievement of going from non-League to the First Division in just ten years is about to occur. Even Northampton couldn't manage that. Then there is this rather odd repeating phenomenon in my career that when I go down, West Ham go up, and when I go up – like this season – the Big Ron will fall.

There have been no more condoms in the bathroom waste bin, and Vivien and I have seen more of each other in the last fortnight than in the previous three months. I'm now starting to think she might have planted it there to get me back on track. I have a momentarily horrible imagining that I ought to have investigated the contents a little more closely to ensure that they were what they appeared to be. They could have been a just a squirt of hand cream. Easier on the nostrils than 10cc of jizz. But then she had gambled correctly that some things wouldn't occur to you on a spontaneous discovery like that one. Not at least until it was too late. I can still think of a few men who would have held on to it to wave in their wives' faces, screaming, 'Now what do you call that?' ('A condom full of sperm, dear.')

As it approached, the final Saturday of the 1985-86 season looked like being one of the most eventful in my life. I wasn't bothered whether Everton or Liverpool won the First Division Championship. That wouldn't be decided until their delayed midweek fixtures, and besides, neither would be going into Europe, whatever happened. My eyes would be on Hammers' last fixture against Aston Villa at Villa Park. Ron's task was simple. He had to make sure his side (37 points) won by three clear goals, whilst at the same time hoping that Ipswich Town (39 points), Manchester City (38 points) and West Bromwich Albion (37 points) all lost. Or as Hurstie put it on the Saturday, 'If I was a shopkeeper in Green Street, I'd cram my warehouse full of slide rules and prayer mats, and book a six week holiday in Barbados'.

Wimbledon had struggled in the last few weeks of the season, gaining only one win and three draws in their last four games, and had been overtaken at the top by Charlton Athletic, the team without a ground, who were top on 74 points, and playing Oldham Athletic at home. Wimbledon were only a point behind, but faced a difficult final away game at Hull City. Third were Portsmouth on 72 points (away to Sunderland) and fourth were Hull City with 71. Just behind them on 70 points were Steve Coppell's Crystal Palace, who had enjoyed a fantastic season since I'd left, racing up the table to within a hair's breadth of a promotion place.

I'd had a phone call from Charlie in the week, who'd told me that he was going to be playing in City's last game at Luton Town, and would I like to drive up and watch him rather than celebrate promotion with my new team? City had been in the news in the last couple of months once relegation threatened, as they hadn't been out of the First Division for twenty years – this famous and successful club – they were last promoted to the First Division the year England won the World Cup. Why had the recently appointed manager (Jimmy Frizzell) recalled Charlie? Though Charlie couldn't see it, it was fairly obvious to me. Nothing

Frizzell had tried since unexpectedly being given the reins from the position of assistant manager had worked. Charlie looked like the last desperate gesture of a man facing defeat.

Charlie had only managed three starts all season, two of these in the Milk Cup, and if I knew him, he wouldn't be match fit. He had sounded something like his old chirpy self on the phone, delighting in telling me how Dave Spick had come up to manage the youth team. That was the first time he'd realised City were genuinely in trouble. With all those seasons of First Division football under his belt, he wasn't sure he was ready to play in the Second Division. He seemed unaware that it might represent a decent swansong, if he could get back in the first team and play a part in mounting a challenge for promotion back to the First Division. He wasn't thinking about that. All he could focus on was winning at Luton Town, and securing that final survival position.

In the end, all the events decreed a change of state for the clubs and people I cared about. Wimbledon went up, pipped to the title by Charlton, but were still the story of the day in the Second Division. The Dons' win over Hull City cleared the way for a clean sweep of London clubs gaining promotion, as Crystal Palace came up on the rails to pip Portsmouth who were well beaten on the day by Sunderland. Big Ron and the Supreme (Cunningham had gone back to Real Madrid and Bobby Barnes was injured) managed a 1-1 draw at Villa Park, though they'd been ahead for most of the game. Ipswich Town were the team that secured a last day reprieve with a 2-0 home win, which meant that despite Charlie leading his team to a fantastic 1-0 victory at Kenilworth Road, City would be in the Second Division next year along with the Wests, Ham and Brom.

To be involved in the management of a First Division team after less than six months as coach was probably the greatest achievement my football career had given me, and to cap it all, I received a runners-up medal as a playing member of the squad. Wimbledon hastily organised a ceremony at the Town Hall, and Vivien and Geoffrey bibbed up to support me at the Awards Evening. I'd never seen GB so proud, and he reassured me that we now had a partnership that could take us to even greater heights. I think it was the booze speaking, but it was nice to hear all the same.

The World Cup Finals in Mexico were something every England fan had been looking forward to since Ron Greenwood had taken over from the half-wits that had been in charge since Alf Ramsey's departure. We all knew as West Ham fans that this might be the best chance England would have for some time to add to our lone World Cup win of 1966.

England knew about the thin air and changing pace of matches from the 1970 World Cup tournament, but football was a very different game now. Players were fitter, and there were many more countries who were producing world class sides ready to complete at the highest level.

England had been drawn in Group F alongside Poland, Portugal and Algeria, and took with them a squad that looked every bit as capable of winning the tournament as the Boys of 66: Goalkeepers: Shilton, Woods, Bailey; Defenders: Stevens, Pearce, Sansom, Martin, Butcher, Anderson, Fenwick; Midfielders: Hoddle, Wilkins, Hateley, Devonshire, Reid, Steven, Hodge; Forwards: Lineker, Waddle, Barnes, Beardsley, Cottee.

Making the news was the omission of the ex-England captain Bryan Robson, who had fallen out with Greenwood over tactics just before Christmas, and the late call-up for 24-year old Nottingham Forest defender Stuart Pearce, who had yet to win an England cap. Tony Cottee's move to Aston Villa earlier in the season and Alan Devonshire's transfer shortly afterwards to Liverpool had meant that both men retained the First Division pedigree that still seemed necessary for admission to the England side.

This tournament was the first World Cup to introduce the idea of a 'penalty shoot-out' that would apply from the knock-out stages. If the score of a game was level after extra time, each side would take five alternate penalties each, and if that didn't produce a winner, it would go to a sudden-death play-off. If West Ham's Ray Stewart had been English, he might have made the squad just for Greenwood to have up his sleeve ready to bring on at the end of an extra-time stalemate.

England saw off Portugal in the first match, without much trouble, 2-0, the goals from Lineker and Waddle. They also beat Algeria, slightly more comfortably, 4-0, with goals from Lineker, Butcher, Hoddle and the substitute Tony Cottee. They then faced Poland, who had won both of their games 2-0, to decide who would have the easier round two game. The winners would face West Germany, the losers Paraguay. A draw and England would top the group on goal difference. It might have been prudent to shove out a second stream team and slum it to the knock-out stages as runners-up, but Greenwood wasn't that kind of man. He put out a full strength side, and finished the group stages as winners with a 1-1 draw, and another goal for Gary Lineker.

155

It was the first time England had faced West Germany in a World Cup tournament game since the final of 1966. Germany were greatly improved as a team, and the European favourites in the tournament, but Greenwood was no mug and had done his homework. He played five men in midfield and four at the back, leaving Gary Lineker as the lone striker. The formation confounded the critics and the pundits back in the television studios, one of whom – Geoff 'Hurstie' Hurst – said that though he still had a great deal of respect for Ron Greenwood, he couldn't see Lineker lasting 90 minutes doing all that running, or imagine how England were going to score.

Hurstie was wrong. The tactics worked like a dream. West Germany had very little of the ball, and whenever they were able to organise a breakaway, Pearce and Stevens cut out any chance of building from the flanks. Karl-Heinz Rummenigge and Dieter Hoeness looked past their best, and when England took the lead just after half time when Stuart Pearce headed home Glenn Hoddle's perfectly-placed corner, the England fans went crazy. The rest of the half was dominated by the presence of Devonshire and Peter Reid, whose tireless running and possession took the last ounce of energy out of the Germans, and England squeezed through.

In the quarter-finals they faced Mexico, who had overcome Bulgaria in the previous round, but despite the home nation having climate and home advantage, England went back to their group stages formation and strolled through with a controlled display of confident football, winning 2-0, the goals scored by Barnes and Reid.

The semi-finals threw a real tough challenge England's way, as they faced Argentina and the brilliance of football's new skill-king Diego Maradona. Maradona and his powerful South American side had virtually destroyed every country they had come up against in the tournament, and were yet to concede a goal. As an added motivator, the political wrangling with the Falkland Islands four years earlier had left bad feelings between the two countries. It would be a difficult game to win.

Greenwood and Lyall worked hard on plans to stifle Maradona's creativity whilst maximising their strength in attack, and in the end gave Tony Cottee a start over Peter Beardsley. Cottee had looked impressive in the two games he had come on in as a substitute, and the power of his running was thought to be a potential match winning ploy. The other semi-final was France against Spain, and most people thought that both of those countries were beatable. The Argentina game became the one to win.

It was wonderful for me watching at home, as Geoffrey had become a football-mad six year old. He wouldn't take his England shirt off, and usually slept in it. We bought him three in the end, so he could rotate them. He could name the squad off by heart, and had his own bean bag football that he kicked ferociously around the front room whenever a match was on.

The day finally came, 25th June 1986. England had only been this far before once in a World Cup, and that was twenty years ago, the year they won it.

What a season. Promotion with my new side, and a year of First Division football ahead of us. If England could bring home the World Cup for the second time, it would revolutionise football. The impact had been seen in 1966, but now we had colour television, giant TVs, slow-motion action replays seconds after each event, and best of all we had … *Saint and Hurstie.*

ITV made a point of trying to outdo the BBC coverage with their star turns, and Hurstie would wind up 'Saint' by referring to Scotland's premature group stage elimination being as a result of their month-long warm-up for the tournament on the Orkney Islands, playing a team of sheep. Another memorable moment was when Hurst spoke about his disallowed goal twenty years earlier, in an interview with Jimmy Greaves, asking if it wasn't about time that the England fans knew the Russian linesman's name was really Greavesovitch. Greaves' retort, that football was 'a funny old game' was punctuated by a shot of Hurst to camera, for once completely bereft of mirth.

The semi-final against Argentina was the most important football match for England in twenty years. The streets were empty five minutes before kick-off, and we all knew we were witnessing something very important, something that could be very good for English football.

The game kicked off at a gentle pace, the moves more like something from a chess game than a frantic competition between athletes. England's captain Terry Butcher had already steered his Ipswich Town team to safety from relegation, and he now looked ready for the bigger challenge.

Cottee's pace ensured that England looked dangerous on the break, but Argentina hadn't earned their reputation as the defensive kings of the tournament for nothing, and the likes of Cuciuffo and Ruggeri kept England chances to a minimum. Stevens and Sansom had dealt with anything Maradona could throw at them until a break just after half-time, where a ball crossed in from the right beat the defence and Maradona climbed high to get a touch before Shilton and turn the ball into the net.

As the crowd erupted, the commentator yelled something about a handball, and sure enough, the swift replay indicated in slow-motion that as Maradona jumped with the keeper it was his hand that had punched the ball beyond Shilton and into the net. Another controversy! Fenwick and Butcher were screaming at the Tunisian referee Ali Bennaceur to consult with his linesman. Despite booking Fenwick for an over-zealous request, the referee finally went over to the linesman, and despite the whistles and baying from the crowd behind him, disallowed the Argentinian goal. He then booked Maradona for cheating, despite a praying display of persecuted martyrdom that would have graced the shrine of any Catholic church.

Unfortunately for England, within four minutes they were genuinely behind to a stunning goal from Maradona who took the ball just inside his own half, and accelerating down the right, took out Alan Devonshire and three defenders to end the move with a perfectly placed low shot, drilled past Shilton with real power. The pictures of Lyall shouting from the dugout over the following twenty minutes clearly demonstrated the sense that these perfect plans for winning the tournament were now under threat. A double substitution replaced Cottee and Reid with Barnes and Waddle on 75 minutes, and England got into gear again. The Argentinians seemed to sense that they had done enough, and Sergio Batista had slowed the game down to almost walking pace as his side controlled the speed of the game. Now all that had gone, Barnes was troubling the defence with his speed, and six minutes after coming on he produced a cross from the left that Gary Lineker got on the end of to equalise and to break the Argentinian defensive tournament record.

Now England sensed victory. Waddle had two shots, the second a terrific effort from 25 yards, brilliantly saved by Pumpido. Barnes continued to take the ball wide, and three minutes from time put over a cross that Lineker missed by inches with the goalkeeper hopelessly out of position. The final whistle indicated a gruelling 30 minutes of extra time. Could England keep pace with the Argentinians, more accustomed to the conditions under pressure? I popped my head outside the front door on my way to make a cup of tea. The street was deserted, but if you listened carefully you could hear the hum of excited chatter across the road as families discussed what might happen in extra time. When I said football was all I had, it remained the truth, even in my last playing days. Nothing could grab you quite like this, player or spectator.

Lyall was out there in the middle with a tray of bottled water, urging on his players, the trainers massaging the tired flesh. One hundred and fifteen thousand people were crammed into that ground. The atmosphere had to be a lifter, no matter how tired you felt as a player.

Shots of the Argentinians showed them to be no less victims of fatigue, and Maradona's face looked frozen into an expression of devastation at the thought of another 30 minutes of running in that heat. The Argentinian manager Carlos Bilardo was barking at his players, raising his hands to express his determination that they should still find the wherewithal to defeat those who would dare to occupy the Falkland Islands. This was a well-quoted comment that Bilardo had made in the days prior to the match.

The heat took its toll in extra time, and no matter how hard the players pushed for the extra ounce of strength to cut in on goal, or connect with a hopeful cross, the chances didn't come, the opportunities weren't there. As the extra time final whistle was blown, the commentator declared, 'So, it's penalties.'

The stadium roared and cheered. The players collapsed in the centre circle. John Lyall came out with his little notebook, scribbling names, checking with the players. At least Barnes and Waddle were out there now. Lineker could take penalties and score all night. Who else was there in the team? Butcher would want to take one. I couldn't think of a fifth taker. Hoddle? Could we do it? Why not? I had seen the French overcome Belgium on penalties in the last round, beating them 4-1. Belgium had missed their first two penalties, missed them – actually put the ball wide – twice! Twelve yards, it can't be that difficult. Charlie had never missed a penalty in a competitive game, from youth team to the first team at Manchester City. He'd been their taker for three years and had scored 12 out of 12. Quite a record. I'd always wandered off when managers had asked, 'Any of you lot take pens?' Did that make me a coward?

Watching now, it was clear that England had won the toss, and would take first. Terry Butcher had the ball and was placing it on the spot. My heart was beating ludicrously fast. Was this a fair way to decide a game? After all the matches and hoping and praying (and playing) to get to this point of a tournament, and then go out on a bad kick? Oh shit.

159

Butcher looks supremely confident. Even the commentator's stopped talking. Then he remembers his job.

'So Butcher, to get England underway in their first ever penalty shoot-out ...'

I watch him take three steps back. Not too far.

'Yes!' An excellent effort, placed low and hard to the keeper's left.

Now Maradona. Little chance of him missing. What's he doing? Wrapping up some toilet paper or something they've thrown onto the pitch. What's the matter with him? *Get on with it you Argentinian Cheat!* Now he's ready.

Oh God, Shilton's saved it! He hit it straight at him, and Shilton's beaten it out!

'He's saved it!' says the commentator, after an eternity.

'Does that mean we're in the final?' Vivien asks. I turn round to see her and Geoffrey, cuddled up, both smiling, on the sofa. I realise I have crawled along the carpet up to within a foot of the screen.

'Not yet,' I say. 'There's a few more to go yet.'

Next up is Gary Lineker. Good move. Two in the bag will really get them on the back foot. I'm not so worried this time and ... He scores. Not as perfectly placed as Butcher's but with more power.

Now it's Batista. No nonsense build-up. He scores easily. The sound seems to have been turned down. I look round for the remote control before I realise it's just the tension of the situation inside the stadium. John Barnes has the ball and is moving towards the spot.

Fresh legs. I want to start chanting it for the necessary effect. But like Batista before him, Barnes wastes no time and slots it home. The replay shows that it went right down the middle, but with the keeper committed, it didn't matter. Now Oscar Ruggeri, the defender who only England have scored a goal against.

He steps back a few paces, and fires the ball home. Three-two.

Now it's Chris Waddle, of Tottenham Hotspur and England. Clever Geordie striker. (Is he a Geordie or a Mackem? Or a Northumberland-ian? I have to shockingly admit, I have no idea) He's a Spur, so dad would have his invisible money on him.

He's skied it! Three, maybe four feet over the bar. He took it too quickly, he should have taken another few steps, got his mind together. Twat. Now the advantage has gone. But so long as we don't miss anoth-er one. He doesn't look too pleased. What was he thinking of?

Next Argentinian. Valdano. The old git. I'm only a year older than him! He's taking a bit more time now, knowing how important the kick has become now we've missed. He steps up and – right in the corner. It's like a stabbing to the heart every one of these penalties, whether they go in or not. Surely some poor spectator somewhere watching this on the telly is going to die.

So it's 3-3 and just one penalty left for each team. Before I can even hazard a guess at who's going to take the last one, I see Stuart Pearce with the ball, making his way towards the spot. Twenty-four years old. I bet that took guts. Why aren't the more experienced players taking it? I look around ... Terry Fenwick, Alan Devonshire, even Glenn Hoddle. Where is he?

Pearce looks horribly nervous. But he looks determined. What kind of a recipe is that? He takes a six pace run up. Bang! Straight at the keeper – he's saved it! Oh no! We were winning this and now if they score ... we're out of the World Cup.

'I've worked it out now,' Vivien says. 'We've lost.'

'Only if he scores,' I say, in desperation.

It's Enrique, one of the younger players. Even younger than Stuart Pearce. What a kick to have to take.

'This to put Argentina into the final,' the commentator barks.

Right in the corner.

Suddenly I can't hear the television. I am heading to the kitchen for a drink. I don't want to watch any more. We're out of the World Cup. On bloody penalties.

I retire as a player at 33 at the end of the following season. GB and I manage our goal of keeping Wimbledon in the First Division. We did it in some style, too, reaching 7th position, with a squad of new and exciting players who were all household names within a few weeks of making their Wimbledon debuts. There were, to name just a few, John Fashanu, a giant of a striker, Lawrie Sanchez, a tricky midfielder and Marcus Gayle, a wiry forward, whose elusive runs and precision finishes were on the end of many of the 62 goals we scored that season. Maybe our club was putting something back into English football after the World Cup semi-final defeat and the miseries of the Heysel Stadium disaster two years previously.

It wasn't such a good year for Charlie. A girlfriend of his, Rachel Everett, who he'd been involved with for six months, died of an accidental drugs overdose, and Charlie was with her when it happened. All he would say was that she'd mixed 'the wrong stuff' and that it was his fault because it was his drink. There was a court case that took weeks to run, and which finally reached a verdict of accidental death, but Charlie was never the same afterwards. He left Manchester City at the end of the season and went to Oldham Athletic. I spent a couple of days up there at the trial, thinking I might offer him some support, but he was inconsolable. I tried to persuade him to come back to London, but he'd already hooked up with an ex-girlfriend who looked like a short cut to something worse. He'd sit in the room smoking and drinking, saying very little. Whenever I spoke about our time together as players or tried to get him to talk about his success at City, he'd clam up or tell me to leave it alone. I took him to one side and told him to call me when he'd sorted things out, but it wasn't a departure filled with hope for better days.

West Ham have hit rock bottom. There follows one of the most dramatic clearouts of talent at a football club that I've ever known. Alan Dickens, a stunningly talented midfielder, on his way to Chelsea. Ray Stewart has gone to Celtic. Mark Dennis has joined Charlton. Keith McPherson has left for Queens Park Rangers.

Billy Bonds became player-coach halfway through the season at the age of 40. He'll be 41 in September, but maybe he is the man for the job. He has the guts and determination that it will take to turn half a squad and a bunch of kids into a side that might be good enough to go up to the First Division and to stay there. The last man to manage that was John Lyall. Pity we couldn't persuade him to come back.

CHAPTER ELEVEN

First of Many

Getting into double figures is an expression that seems designed for everything except age. There is something terrifying about acknowledging that every time you are asked to fill out a form you will now need to write two digits until the day you die. If you ever need to write three, you'll either have a nurse to do it for you, or you'll just organise a fecal signature on the sheet to let them know you're still alive.

It is Geoffrey's tenth birthday. Geoff's, actually. I've been calling him 'Geoff' for the last three weeks so he can get acclimatised to his new name, but it hasn't been that much of a transition as I've been the only one calling him Geoffrey for the last three years.

We're still in Wimbledon, a couple of extensions bigger, but no need to move out to the shires yet. Gary left the club at the end of last season to work for a satellite company, Sky. It is a little absurd however to talk about 'a' satellite company; there is only one. There were two for a while, but then they merged, and the smaller one has already lost its name off the company logo, almost as if it had never existed.

The company needed a couple of 'big names' from the world of football to back its launch, and you don't get much bigger than Gary as far as football management is concerned. He took 'Little Wimbledon' to their biggest triumph in 1988, when we won the FA Cup at Wembley. Little Lawrie Sanchez scored the only goal in our 1-0 win over the Mighty Liverpool. It may yet prove to be the last David beats Goliath contest in the history of football. We shall see.

If I thought football had changed in the eighties, the first four months of the nineties have served as something of a counter-revolution. English teams were finally readmitted into Europe, after FIFA had become tired of beating back the weekly faxes of complaint from the chairmen of the rich clubs in the First Division. First Division? If ITV's television supremo Greg Dyke had had his way, there would have been a 'Super League' breaking free of the rest of the English clubs, going off to play football on their own, and not sharing their ball with anyone else. Though he didn't get his wishes, ITV still secured exclusive rights to the Football League matches. The BBC were wiped out with one stroke of a pen. My father would have been delighted.

What no-one in the public knew at the time was that there might as well have been a 'Super League' as ITV had pronounced a behind closed doors 'gentlemen's agreement' that they would only show main games that featured the 'Top Five'. These were at the time thought to be Manchester United, Liverpool, Everton, Arsenal and Tottenham. No room for 'Little Wimbledon' then.

I've only been the manager since last October, but I am learning fast. The main thing that has changed since I was a young player is the arrival of The Agent. Footballers' wages have begun creeping up since the investment of the television shilling into football. It's hard to complain as they are the ones playing it, and the ones whose industry decides the fortunes of the various clubs. However, though they may claim their 'clients' are better off with them minus ten per cent than without them and in a straightjacket contract, this new evolutionary leech is slowly beginning to exercise control over the raw material in the game. Agents started off as dads with an inflated sense of self-worth, unemployed mates, chancers, scumbag shysters, failed plumbers and – and these were the only ones I was never too critical of – players whose careers had been cut short through injury. They would accompany their client to contract discussions (that they had usually initiated) with faces like eighteenth century priests, more likely to shake their head than to nod it. As the manager of Wimbledon, I didn't spend that much time with players' agents. I would usually offer them two alternatives for negotiation: 'nothing' or 'still nothing'. But these were early days, and I knew sooner or later that I would be locking horns with one of them.

Geoff is not a bit like his father. Actually, he might well be like his father for all I know, but he's nothing like me. For a start, he's very much a social individual. You won't catch him spending more than a minute on his own if he can help it. He's always out with his mates, and very rarely brings them home. It's difficult to say whether that's to do with embarrassment about the people he lives with, or the fact that he just loves being outside. He doesn't tell anyone what I do, like many kids would, and he's not even that bothered about coming to the ground on match days if we're playing at the weekend. I don't invite him to the weekday matches because of school. School takes precedence over every other part of his life. There are educational and financial reasons for that. After much deliberation, we sent him to the local private school that's just a couple of minutes walk from the house. I am naturally a little worried that he'll end up with a plummy brogue, but that doesn't seem to be happening. For some reason I've yet to fathom, he's begun to talk with an accent that sounds vaguely Australian.

Vivien let's him get on with it. So long as he puts his stuff away and keeps his room tidy, she doesn't get on his case. She's actually an excellent mother, and at home I often feel like a leg of pork at a barmitzvah. The belief is that you should spend as much time with your children as you can when they're growing up, but Geoff doesn't seem to have read that book. But he does love football. He's always out playing with his mates, and is a striker in the local League team, regularly knocking in goals for them. I'm not allowed to watch, though I usually pop round with the binoculars to a neighbour's house that overlooks the playing fields. Geoff's a big lad, already very strong in the tackle, and looks a couple of years older than his age. We'll see how well he does when the others catch up.

Despite the money that continues to come into the game from the ITV deal, English football is in a major mess. After the glory of a semi-final place in the 1986 World Cup, the national team qualified for the 1988 European Championships and exited swiftly after three draws. An early departure and yet they hadn't been beaten. It certainly felt like a defeat with only two goals scored over the three matches. A World Cup tournament in Italy should have been the revival motivator. It wasn't. In an oversized qualifying group that featured a herd of European nations halfway through emerging from forty-five years of communist rule, England have failed to reach the competition finals altogether.

And just as the European ban from the Heysel Stadium disaster was lifted, an afternoon of FA Cup carnage at Hillsborough has led to calls for all seater stadiums. The fences erected at the ground as a result of the Heysel hooliganism were on that day one of the main factors in a death toll of 96 that is likely to change the way people watch football for years to come. Just when there's lots of money coming into football – supposedly – we haven't seen any of it – great piles of cash are going to have to be found to put every spectator in a seat.

165

It is quite clever in a way, as crowds have been falling again over the last two years. With less room for fans because of more seats, the clubs can charge more, have less fans and still fill up the grounds. It is a little hard not to be cynical about it. Plough Lane can only hold just over 9,500 on the terraces. With seats, we'll be lucky to get enough space for 5,000 at home matches.

The FA met as a response to an official report presided over by Lord Justice Taylor after the Hillsbrough disaster to make several high profile decisions about football. They missed the opportunity to ban players' agents from the game, but they did recommend identity cards for fans and all seater stadiums. In theory, it will make football stadiums safer, but there will be many other effects as a result that are certain to change the face of football forever in this country.

Billy Bonds is one face that hasn't changed. He is still manager of West Ham United. Loyal, determined, thoughtful and strategically sound in his planning, Bonds lacks just one final ingredient. Money. They are beginning to call it the final piece of the jigsaw in many clubs up and down the land, but West Ham's piece seems to have got hidden behind the club sofa. Bonds was actually closest to promotion in his very first season as manager where, despite half the side leaving the club almost overnight, he still had a few players who could get results when they all played well together.

In the end it wasn't quite good enough, and they missed out on one of the new Play-Off places by just two points. Three years later, and it's another 'just above mid-table' finish. Although I still got to games when I was at Palace and assistant manager of Wimbledon on 'scouting missions', I've only been twice to see West Ham this season. The first time was to their youth team ground at Little Heath to check out a fourteen year old local youngster of theirs called David Beckham. Bonds secured his signature over the heads of many other managers, including Manchester United's Brian Kidd. Beckham was clearly talented, but I couldn't make my mind up about him, though I was very impressed on my next visit by a kid in the reserves in his early twenties called Dean Holdsworth. We bought him at the end of January, and he's already scored eight goals for the club in just ten games.

By the end of the season it's an overdue break after a boring World Cup. The tournament's only redeeming feature is that Italy don't win it in front of their fans, and are eclipsed in the semis by the Germans. They play for the last time as West Germany in a historically dull final decided by a single goal (and a penalty at that) over an even duller Argentina.

One thing about football is that you always have the following season to look forward to, whatever went before, no matter how bad. It's another chance that your team might win the league / sack the crap chairman / win one of the lesser trophies for a back door entry into Europe / go into administration / find a brilliant player who will play a handful of games before signing for Liverpool / move grounds to somewhere that's too far away to get to / finally get the new stand finished and rake up season ticket prices. At least these were the kind of choices teams were offering in the 1980s. This new decade was an unknown entity, and as technology was advancing, so was the fear that soon every professional game would be televised and nobody would attend the matches any more. But that couldn't really happen. There was no substitute for actually being at the game, was there?

A very significant event of the early 90s was the death of Bobby Moore from cancer. Always an ambassador for the game, and the legendary captain of West Ham United's Championship winning side in 1972-73, Moore died just three months short of the twentieth anniversary of the event, and in the first programme of matches on the Saturday following his death, at all the grounds in the Football League where games were being played, there was a minute's silence in memory of the great man. I was reminded of my childhood, and the good fortune I had experienced to be watching football at a time when Bobby Moore was playing at the height of his skills and fame. We'd lost Gordon Banks from that team, and now Bobby Moore. I got hold of a poster of Moore, Peters, Wilson and Greaves from the 1966 World Cup Final, Moore up on their shoulders, holding that tiny trophy aloft. A truly great footballer.

It seemed just the blinking of an eye before a satellite company crept out of the dark shadows of the abandoned television edit suites to stretch its new financial legs and raise itself up to its full colossal height. Despite the shite 1990 World Cup, there had been a major investment in football by the suits in glass towers with their promise of sophisticated computerised recording equipment and wall-to-wall match coverage.

ITV had begun to dominate football, but had become complacent and worse, boring. The stunning decision to axe Saint and Hurstie after five years was part of the larger dehumouridifying of football. With the amount of money that was now being ploughed into the game, something had to give, and the first casualty was humour. The intentional kind, anyway. There was still plenty to laugh at, like Martin Tyler's jumpers or the sudden predilection for Scottish football summarisers at live games. The spirit, however, had been tugged out of football's writhing financially anorexic body, leaving it dependent on the meat and drink of the nineties, sponsorship.

1992-93 was the launch season for The Primary Football League. It sounded a bit like a competition played by nine and ten year olds, but like anything, once it had been repeated enough on television and on billboards, it began to sound normal. ITV had axed Saint and Hurstie, but within two years it had fallen foul of the satellite shekel and was now on its hands and knees, looking on the floor for crumbs of comfort that might on closer inspection come to resemble a half decent programming idea.

The new Primary League featured a change to the number of teams in the top division which went down to just eighteen. To make the adjustment virtually overnight meant that sixteenth spot, traditionally a relatively comfortable position for clubs just hanging on to their top flight status, now became relegation position one of nine. It was decided that the Second Division, which was now going to be called Pontins Division One, couldn't be denied its three promotion places to the new Primary League, and so after the end of season's play-offs, the team who had finished sixth in the old Second Division, Sunderland, who won the play-offs, replaced Everton, the team who had finished sixteenth in the old First Division. It was a novel way to play musical chairs with the league positions, but for those who were sick and tired of Everton escaping relegation by the skin of their teeth for the last seven years, it made a kind a cruel sense.

Wimbledon FC were never likely to raise sufficient cash to turn Plough Lane into an all-seater stadium, despite promised European grants and an all-weather collection bucket outside the ground, so after several meetings with interested franchises, an agreement was made with Brentford for an indefinite ground sharing scheme. Though Brentford were in the New IKEA Second Division (old Royal Bank of Scotland Third Division), their sponsors, His Highness Sheikh Rahkhoum bin Rashid Al Rakhoum of Dubai, had financed a new 40,000 capacity all-seater stadium that was currently being built in Osterley, in West London. In the meantime, as all clubs had two seasons to organise playing in an all-seater stadium, Wimbledon would stay at Plough Lane until 1994-95, when the ground would be ready.

We had finished thirteenth in the First Division in 1991-92, our second best ever end to a season, but we'd missed relegation by just five points.

The theme tune of The Primary League that was played as teams came out on to the pitch before every Primary League game was, not unpredictably, Primal Scream's 'Movin' On Up'. And so what had been quite a pleasant pop tune that you might tap your fingers on the steering wheel to on the way to work became the kind of incessant Nazi braindance that had led to high profile suicides, international incidents and military coups.

The other issue with satellisation, was the need to identify yourself as one of them by the erection of a small black dish on the side of your house. If your dwelling was north facing, you could hide the carbuncle on the back of your house, above the extension, and cover it with some artificial creepers or a pantomime trellis. If you were north facing, then you had to make the decision. Do I care what my neighbours think of me? This problem might be solved for you if your neighbours had all 'dished up', in which case following suit wasn't too difficult. If you lived on litterless estates where even unshut gates were frowned upon, you'd have to go down the pub to watch the football. And it did mean people were going to the pub now to do more than drink. Now they could go down to their local to complain about the number of satellite dishes that had gone up all over the estate, and wasn't it shocking?

By the beginning of the 1994-95 season, all of us at the club were ready for the Big Move to Osterley. The die-hard fans were staging an 'alternative opening to the season' with an Old Wimbledon XI facing some other medleyed opposition of show biz stars and football wannabies in the long grass at Plough Lane. The truth was, it was a brick-ended wreck of a ground that hadn't really been good enough even for Third Division football. The times they were a-Changing, and it didn't take me long to realise once I'd seen it, that the Osterley Ground was a fantastic improvement on what we'd known.

I'd been at the club for just over four years, and in that time we'd finished fourteenth, thirteenth, fifteenth and twelfth. Not bad for a team with a squad of just twenty first teamers. My goal had been to hold on until we got to our new shared stadium, and now we'd made it. Most people, especially those in satellite world, hated us, because we represented the old unglamorous days of football. For the last three home games at Plough Lane in 1993-94, the opposition were put up in a local Wimbledon hotel and bussed down to the ground, once they'd changed. We made a point of staying put amongst the smell of carbolic and weed killer.

Despite the crass Americanisation of our beloved national sport 'soccer', some interesting by-products had squeezed out from between the paving stones and discarded satellite dishes. With a more visible stage, and identity card schemes, football grounds now seemed safer places. People could go to matches wearing their team's colours, and even though the tribal atmosphere at grounds from the sixties, seventies and eighties had almost disappeared, the sight of a wall of fans all wearing their side's first team shirt, was an emotional experience and motivational for the players. What you saw now as a player was almost as important as what you heard.

The 1994 World Cup was another disaster for England. They reached third position in the qualifiers in their group of six, but with the highest points total and goals scored, still reached one of the wild card place play-offs, where they faced Latvia over two legs. The England side was now managed by Ron Atkinson, who had followed his disastrous eighteen months at West Ham with a surprisingly successful managerial spell at Leeds United. He was one of the first managers to welcome foreign internationals into his side, and as a result got the jump over the majority of other clubs. His Leeds side had won the last First Division Championship by seven clear points after only two seasons back in the top league.

Big Ron had also smartened up his act and hired a professional hypnotist to tone down his language, and paid a personal elecutioneer to work on his accent. Favourite expressions like 'early doors' and 'back stick' were abandoned and Ron courted praise at the highest level for his new found measured comments on television programmes like *Question Time* and *Newsnight*. The FA were persuaded and halfway through 1993-94 he was offered the job after Graham Taylor was sacked.

Within five months his England team faced Latvia at Wembley in the first leg of the Wild Card play-off. Ron had tidied up his act as a speaker, but his England side played poorly, managing just three shots on goal on that Wednesday evening in late March, in a game that finished 0-0. Latvia didn't manage a single corner. In the second leg a fortnight later, England striker Paul Gascoigne missed a first half penalty, but had the chance to take it again when the referee adjudged the goalkeeper to have moved. His second effort struck a post and went wide. As Oscar Wilde might have put it, to miss one penalty, Mr Gascoigne, may be regarded as a misfortune, to miss two makes you and 'Big Posh-Speaking Ron' look like prize wankers. In the last minute of the first half, Latvia's striker Aleksandrs Stolcers hit a speculative shot from twenty yards that England keeper Peter Shilton somehow allowed to creep under his body for a goal that proved the winner on the night. So, despite the Football League being more Americanised than ever before, the 1994 World Cup tournament was played in The United States without the accompanying presence of an England team.

As for West Ham, the unthinkable. Not the departure of Billy Bonds, which he made with his customary grace and loyalty, acknowledging that seven years of old Second / new First Division football was enough trying, thanks. Not even the subsequent appointment of the untried or tested assistant manager Alan Devonshire. At least not at first. And at least it was the appointment of someone who knew – and had once walked away from – the set-up at West Ham.

The 1993-94 season was something of a watershed for the Hammers. Devonshire had returned to Upton Park having played under Bonds throughout the 1992-93 season and, much to the surprise of the press pack, had been given the reins in the close season after Bonds' farewell announcement. As a 37 year old, Devonshire was one of the youngest managers in the football league, but the domestic and European Championships he had won at Liverpool showed the calibre of the player that the West Ham Board were relying on to get them out of trouble. It was a massively popular appointment with the fans who had always loved 'Devs' and who hadn't forgotten the quality of his performance in the FA Cup Final of 1980 and his part in the 1980-81 record points promotion season.

Devonshire could actually take some credit for the team he started the season with, as two of the signings had been on his recommendation (Collymore from Southend and Beauchamp from Oxford United), but if he or anyone else thought it was a West Ham side capable of gaining promotion after seven failed years of effort from Billy Bonds, who was no fool, they were mistaken.

Devonshire's 1993-94 First XI: Les Sealey, Kenny Brown, Julian Dicks, Steve Potts, Colin Foster, Mitchell Thomas, Clive Allen, Kevin Keen, Stan Collymore, Martin Allen, Joey Beauchamp. Substitute: George Parris.

Julian Dicks had just returned from an extended knee injury, which had probably saved West Ham from being forced to sell him to one of the many Primary League clubs who were waiting in the wings to get him on their books. He was a defender very much in the Mark Dennis mould, committed, brave and skilful. The defence was always better off with him than without him. He also possessed a powerful shot that was worth nine or ten goals a season. Could Devonshire persuade him to stay at the club?

Stan Collymore was another important player in the side, strong, dextrous and cunning, he had found goals easy to come by in the new First Division. Joey Beauchamp made and scored spectacular goals, and his real strength was in his weak, wimpish appearance that belied his power in the tackle and intelligent reading of the game. Clive Allen was a workhorse of a journeyman, and would always score goals. His cousin Martin was a strong attacking midfield player, but likely to leave if Devonshire didn't improve on Bonds' achievements. Other than that, the side were just another good First Division outfit, no worse or better than the others on paper. They needed leadership or the ability to gel like a mediocre West Ham side had never gelled before if gaining promotion was to be a serious option.

The gel turned out to be KY Jelly and turned to water fairly quickly. Collymore went to Nottingham Forest at Christmas, and Beauchamp left for Ipswich Town the following month. Devonshire used the money to buy Simon Webster from Charlton, Mark Pembridge from Derby and an ageing Leroy Rosenior from Fulham. Webster broke his leg in training before he'd even played a game, Pembridge spent the rest of the season unable to command a place, and Rosenior only played half the games because of an old recurring groin injury. Devonshire had spent a career completely devoid of injuries, but it seemed that he had no luck as a manager with any of the players he signed.

The others in the squad weren't far short of dismal. The days when a claret and blue shirt might have meant more than a footballer's wage had clearly gone. The home form was adequate, but once the team bus headed away from the Barking Road, the team seemed to all put on losing boots. They managed only two wins away from home all season, though one of those was against champions-to-be Newcastle United. By the time the final game came around, home to Charlton Athletic, it was all a foregone conclusion, West Ham were going into the Third Division of the Football League (never mind that they now called it the Second) for the first time in their illustrious history, and in the season before a hundred years of West Ham football was to be celebrated. The New Second Division. What a place for the ex-champions of the Football League to be spending their centenary year. By the time Charlton had finished things off with a 1-0 win – their goal I noticed with some irony scored by an ex-Crystal Palace player Alan Pardew – West Ham really were bottom of the table.

	P	W	D	L	F	A	Pts
20 Notts Co	46	10	21	15	48	62	51
21 Luton	46	13	11	22	50	64	50
22 Cambridge	46	13	10	23	52	71	49
23 Bristol C	46	11	16	19	48	69	49
24 West Ham	46	10	12	24	55	87	42

This was my team, the team I'd followed for 28 years, sunk like a boat chained to the World Trade Centre. While this was happening, the tiny Wimbledon FC continued to survive in the Primary League in a shared ground and with a professional history of just eighteen years. There was little to adequately explain the phenomenon, and it seemed certain now that the construction of the final part of the new stadium at Upton Park and its several million pound new West Stand would be put on hold for another year. Teams below the new First Division were under no immediate pressure to go all-seater until the year 2000. This famous old East London club had reached the lowest point in its history, in my own lifetime.

I wasn't wallowing in despair, though. My wages were linked to the success of the club I was at, and although this wasn't Liverpool FC, having GB at Sky Sports meant I had more control over my press conferences and after match interview pieces than probably any other manager in the Primary League. I was in the perfect position as a manager. People in the business assumed that there was no money at Wimbledon, so there wasn't anyone coveting my job. All I had to do was keep the side in the top league and I'd be fine. Unless I wasn't happy doing that. Unless I wanted to go elsewhere.

My house was paid for, and I had the flat in Clapham which was now worth a small fortune. I was keeping it for Geoff, but that was a situation that might require some expert handling. So far as Vivien knew, I had sold it when we bought the house back in 1981. There are good lies and bad lies. There are intelligent lies and stupid lies. There are also lies that start off as good lies but turn out to be bad ones. It would be hardly credible that I should buy back the very same flat that I used to own. Geoff was a year old when I 'sold' it. He wouldn't remember being there, though there are photos of him in his cot and of the three of us together on Clapham Common.

Geoff had gone for trials with Leyton Orient and Charlton, the latter set up by GB, the former as a direct result of him being spotted playing for his not-so little league team. Both wanted him, but in the end he came to Wimbledon. Keith Peacock, a Charlton scout and senior coach, asked me why I hadn't taken him on myself.

'You got kids, Keith?'

'Two girls.'

'And if you had a boy ...'

'If he was good enough, of course I'd have him at Charlton. You've got all that experience to give him, Roy. You'd be mad to let him go somewhere else.'

'I don't want him to feel he owes me anything. That's a fucking burden to carry round with you all your life. There's always the risk one day that I'll say to him, if it wasn't for me ...'

'If it wasn't for you he wouldn't even be here.'

'Yeah,' I said. 'You've got a point.'

He wouldn't be here if it wasn't for me. Keith was right there. Whether or not I was his father, I still had some kind of a creative role in his life, even as a catalyst.

Geoff came to Wimbledon in the end. Once I asked him, he said 'yes' straight away. And yet he had rarely been interested in the club when he first started playing football. I introduced him to Dave Spick on the Monday. Yeah, I know, I haven't always been a fan of Dave 'this ain't smiling, I've got wind' Spick, but he's actually got quite a record for producing great players through the youth team. It's only all these years later that I realise what he did for me at Palace, how I still use a lot of training techniques that he used to use back then. Not that he'd ever call them 'techniques'.

Our youth team academy is based at a local independent school's training ground. I got myself on the Board of Governors there a couple of years ago and made them an offer they couldn't refuse. It's a kind of legitimate tax dodge, but it means the school wins with the facilities, and we don't have to pay tax on the building. Everyone's happy.

Once I got linked up with the careers officer in Merton we could have the kids doing half a week's work experience and the other half with us. We only have to shell out half their salary. If they're good enough, we sign them. If not, they might end up at Carshalton Athletic or Sutton United. It's a little industry that's working nicely. Dave seems happy with it, anyway. He's actually got quite a sense of humour after all, old Spicksy.

There is only one thing in my life that I'd like to get rid of, and that's agents. One of them, let's call him Shyster Arsehole, has three of my players on his books, as well as two at Chelsea. He called a meeting a few days into the New Year to let me know that the three are looking to make what the two are making, and how long is it before I can make that happen. The one thing I will say about him is at least we have these meetings alone, without the players there to start getting ahead of themselves.

'There are a few things I can make happen, but none of them are likely to improve the salary of your clients.'

'They're top quality players, Roy. They could go anywhere, but they stay here. Isn't it about time you started rewarding that kind of loyalty.'

That's another word that is over-used. Loyalty. Some of these kids wouldn't know loyalty if it shat in their laps.

'This is Wimbledon, not Real Madrid. Their weekly wages could buy them a new car every fortnight with enough change to rent a flat in Holland Park. When I was playing, it took the best part of a year to save up for those kind of expenses. And we didn't have agents to raise our profile with the manager in the name of greed. It wouldn't have occurred to us.'

'Man of your talent, born too early. You missed out, Roy.'

'It's your boys who are missing out. Take them to Chelsea if Chelsea wants them. They're all on contracts that someone'll have to buy their way out of. They'll get a wage rise next year in line with how high we finish. Tell them to play better. Now bugger off.'

That guy was one of the decent ones, believe it or not. But I won't row with them. I've actually started letting my assistant Tommy talk to them. He's shrewd, nods and says yes all the time. Yes, I agree with you, you're right. Then when the money question comes up, it's I'll check with Roy and get back to you. Divide and rule. Old-fashioned but effective.

Having said that, two out of three are at Chelsea by the time the next transfer window opens. Still, we got a decent contract-breaking pay-off that should get me a young centre-back from one of the lower league teams. At that level, they'll come anywhere if it means top league football.

So, we've managed to stay up for another season. Fifteenth again, like the year before last. We were safe a few weeks before the end of the season, so went and lost the last three games. The position looks worse than the way we finished the year, but when people look back, they'll say 'another narrow escape'. That team, holding on, waiting for the inevitable. And when they go down it'll be Plummet Airlines. I hear a lot of that, but I don't argue. If it ever happens I don't want the 'told you so' merchants wagging fingers and accusing me of having spent my life 'in denial'.

A week after we've broken up for the season, I celebrate my 41st birthday. We have a few guests round, some friends of Vivien, a few come from the club, even some of Geoff's mates. The house is packed, but as I'm standing up in the corner, listening to one of Alan Curbishley's jokes, I realise that if I ever had any friends, well they're not here. Chloe, I haven't seen her since 1990. Gary I only see at Sky on a Friday, he rarely comes out in the evenings. And then there's Charlie.

Gary got Charlie a job reporting on matches in the week and on Saturdays. He had a few business interests in Manchester, but he sold them, sold his house and moved down to London. He just had enough to get a flat. When I think what this guy was earning at City in the early eighties. The money from Sky was keeping him going fairly comfortably at first, and Gary said he seemed to enjoy the banter with the other players in the studio. Three months in, he had his first heart attack. This is a forty year old man, so part of that history has gone to places that I don't even know about. My mate, Charlie. The guy who was twenty times as talented as me, and who got me that trial at Crystal Palace.

He was recuperating, then seven weeks later he has another attack. He doesn't have anyone; wife, girlfriend, kids … He wouldn't take anyone on after Rachel died.

Gary's persuaded Sky to continue paying his salary, and they're doing it, thank God. There must be a few people working there with hearts.

It's now been two months since the second attack, and they think he'll be alright. They say both attacks were only minor, but there doesn't seem anything particularly minor to me about having a heart attack when you're forty. It's his birthday next month. He's five weeks younger than me. Before Curbishley can finish the joke, I wander out into the hall to give Charlie a ring.

Chapter Twelve

They think it's all over – it isn't ...

There comes a time in our lives when we have drained all the fight and the anger out of our system, when running up or down the stairs is a distant memory. When the sound of a hairdryer evokes nostalgia. This is the time when we can finally settle down and enjoy our lives. You see couples in their later years, talking over fences, no more thoughts about getting their leg over anything other than an aspidistra. But then why should I suddenly start thinking about all of this? I'm only 45 ...

He turned up at the house when Vivien was away. I don't know how he got the address, and I'm not going to ask him. I remembered him the moment I saw his face, though he seemed a little unsure about me at first. What is he, some kind of an idiot? Who else my age would be answering the door of this house? How has he found out where we live?

I let him in and make him a cup of tea. He waits until he's taken a sip before announcing what he's here about.

'I want to see him,' he says.

'There he is. On the mantelpiece. In his kit. That was when he made his debut last season.'

'I mean in the flesh.'

'Simon, isn't it?' He nods, absently. 'Is this some kind of a mid-life crisis that brought you here, or are you just slow by nature? I thought you and Vivien sorted this out.'

'He's twenty years old, tomorrow. Can't I see him? You don't have to tell him who I am.'

'Look at the photo, Simon. He's not your son. Look, you can take it.' I've picked up the frame and am offering it to him.

'I don't want it. I just want the chance to see him.'

'And if I give you that chance, you'll go away? And never come back?'

His eyes show he is clearly comforted by the offer, but he doesn't say anything.

'You wait here.'

I rush out to my jacket pocket, and return to the front room where I've left him, imagining momentarily that by now he'll be rifling through the drawers, looking for something incriminating. He isn't. He's sitting in my chair by the window. Cheeky git.

'There,' I say, handing him the envelope. 'The Harry Curtis stand, Lower Tier. 3.00 next Saturday. You've got 90 minutes if he doesn't get subbed or sent off. And quite honestly, that's more than you deserve. It's a £25 ticket, so make sure you use it.'

I show him to the door, and in a couple of minutes it's all over.

I look up at the clock and realise I've been playing with this thing for nearly two hours. The first mobile phones were just like, well … phones, but this one stores numbers, addresses, birth dates, appointments … It's come along just in time, before my thinking matter turns to sludge. I can't fall behind with this stuff. I gave up with music when I was 40, but that was more about taste than fashion, though they're probably distant cousins.

I have a feeling that Wimbledon's tenure in the Primary League might be coming to an end. With five games to go, Watford are pretty much down, but there are four teams fighting over the last two relegation places. This is after the league went back up to twenty teams in 1998-99. It's between us, Bradford City, Sheffield Wednesday and Leeds United. Three from Yorkshire and the cockney minnows fighting for two survival places in the twenty-first century. Actually, only people from north of the Watford Gap would call Wimbledon 'cockneys'. It's become a lazy and ludicrous short hand journalistic term for any team who play in a ground with a London postcode. We actually train in Surrey, so even by their dim-witted etymology, we can only really be termed 'semi-cockneys'.

Tommy Jenner, my assistant, has already told me he doesn't want the manager's job. I made a suggestion that I would call it a day if we go down. I would probably resign after the general furore and once the

178

dust had begun to settle. As I told him, if he then stepped in, we might still hang on to a few of our good players to give it a real go next season. I offered to stay on in some kind of advisorial capacity – that's what they call easy money just for being on the end of a phone all day – but Tom's three years older than me, and has given me the 'When you go, I go' mindset. A rare bit of loyalty (or justifiable cowardice) in the circumstances.

This club now feels as much like my football home as Palace ever did. Last October they rolled out the red carpet with a fantastic evening at the Town Hall, with the Mayor, the Local MP, the Fan Club and all the old players from the amateur days. Ten years in the top flight as manager. Though we're one of the youngest League sides, we have been in that top division for fourteen years. Even though we were forced to leave Plough Lane, we've actually been made to feel at home at Osterley Park, and the fanbase and average attendances have even climbed slightly over the last five years, despite the crass inequalities of the Primary League.

The improving attendance figures are probably a knock-on national effect from England qualifying for the 1998 World Cup, and subsequently reaching the quarter-finals. Despite going out on penalties again, as they did in 1986, at least it was to the eventual winners France, who played brilliantly throughout the competition.

Sky Sports now cover events like the England Toddlers Under-18 month championships at Wembley Mothercare. Just put the prefix 'England' before any event, and those Sky cameras will be there with their customary nine spectators to ensure that the event is televised worldwide. Great if you're an ex-pat out in Alice Springs, desperate for a dose of mother country culture; not so good if you're the parent of a football-crazed bunch of obese kids who won't leave their patch in front of the telly for fear that they might miss something. Yes, kids, you're missing your life. There it goes, outside the house, passing you by.

I spent a Sunday with Charlie in the close season, having a lunchtime drink by the river in Kingston. The hospital was right. He has made a fantastic recovery, but he's not quite the same. His speech occasionally slurs, and Sky have had complaints saying they shouldn't let children see drunks on television before the watershed. Charlie is never drunk on a broadcast day. GB will send a minder over to 'get some shopping for him'. Although there might be a run down to the shops for some fags and a newspaper, the minder will be a trusted runner whose job it is to chat with him about whatever he wants to talk about on the day, and then to drive him up to Sky and back. Up to now it's been working okay. I make a regular contribution to Charlie's 'Tesco run fund' as Gary calls it. Whether it's my conscience tweaking or an acknowledgement that I owe this man, it doesn't matter. We've read enough about post-football syndrome to know that the support of friends is always a significant part of many ex-players finding the wherewithal to lead a safe and comfortable life.

Charlie doesn't say much, but he laughs a lot at my reminiscences. There is a particularly desperate story about the time when he was making out with Gerry O'Donnell's girlfriend on match days. O'Donnell was a burly Republic of Ireland striker whose arrival signalled the beginning of the end for Charlie as an automatic City selection. Unable or unwilling to raise his game to fight for his place back, Charlie did the next best thing and put his energy into tracking down O'Donnell's girlfriend and showing her a bit of form. Thankfully finding her proved the only difficulty, and with a nose like a bloodhound, that wasn't going to pose too many problems for him. Targeting the dimmest of the girls in the Press Office, he said O'Donnell's girlfriend was planning a surprise birthday for him, and he'd been put in charge of finding the venue. Could he have her number to let her know the details? If she'd just checked the fact that O'Donnell's birthday had come and gone in the previous month, she might have thwarted Charlie's plan. As it was, she gave Charlie one of O'Donnell's girlfriend's business cards (she sold exotic items to groups of women at lingerie house parties) and he gave her a call. With his legendary smooth talk, Charlie was soon trying out Yvonne's full range of items. He even found out what 'love balls' were, and how to use them to maximum effect.

Charlie decided that they could only meet when O'Donnell was in the starting line-up and he wasn't playing or on the bench. He even rented a house two blocks from the ground in the hope that both he and O'Donnell could score simultaneously and have their achievements saluted by the roar of the fans.

It all went pear-shaped during a midweek Littlewoods Cup tie (same League Cup / different sponsors) away to Stockport County, which he had been told that morning he wouldn't be in the squad for. He'd quickly set up an evening jaunt with Yvonne once he'd heard the game would be covered live on the radio. He was breaking his own rules, but the idea of having the radio on quietly in the background with O'Donnell's name being mentioned periodically, while he was banging his girlfriend, appealed to Charlie. Yvonne made so much noise that she was unlikely to hear anything Radio City's commentator might be saying. Nevertheless, when the commentary started and the team lists were read out, Charlie realised that, if he wasn't very much mistaken, the name 'Barth' had been mentioned in the list of City subs. In spite of the close attention he was receiving, Charlie sat up, grabbed his coat and said, 'I'm playing for City!' belted down the stairs, leapt into his car and drove off, never to show his face there again.

Charlie had told that story so many times, that it was easy for me to recount, particularly with the punch line that, 'as far as she knew up to then, I worked for the DHSS!'

I always find imagining the expression on her face the thing that makes me laugh the most about that story.

Charlie confided in me that he had been seeing one of the girls who worked for Sky and whose dad was a mad City fan. I didn't say anything, but I kept my fingers crossed that he wouldn't decide to tell her his Gerry O'Donnell story in a moment of weakness.

The twenty-first century promises to view football through widescreen eyes as a competition dominated by a handful of clubs that the rest of the country can merely gaze at longingly from their safe concrete edge of town stadiums. The whole family are welcome to sit on a piece of moulded plastic, surrounded by 5,000 other people wearing the club's home strip and Mexican Waving to each other. I have grown with it, even celebrated the partial demise of hooliganism that its inception has heralded, but I wonder how things might have been without Heysel or Hillsbrough.

They sat on the stone steps in Athens and Ancient Rome. Jesus probably sat when he watched the disciples have a kick-about in front of the local temple. There have never been terraces at cricket matches, other than the section in front of the Tavern. The Americans and Australians have always had all-seater stadiums for their sports. And there you have it. The terraces are very much an English invention and institution. You just have to accept however that there aren't the fans around to fill them again, apart from in Newcastle and Manchester, even if they were to bring them back.

At least football has continued to entertain the world through its occasionally active political dimension. As the middle class's new plaything, Prime Minister Tony Blair in a radio interview made sure he spoke rapturously about his days as a fan sitting behind the goal at St James' Park, watching Newcastle striker Jackie Milburn. Which he could have done if his dad had taken him there when he was four, and if they'd had a seven foot high seat put on the terraces for him to sit on.

Even at Wimbledon we get the Government's Press Office ringing us up for free tickets when Liverpool, Chelsea, Manchester United or Arsenal are in town. No callers for Bradford City, I was surprised to note. The chairman insists we hand them out whenever we're asked for them, presumably just in case someone can be persuaded to tell Merton Council to give us some land to build a proper ground on. It hasn't happened yet, needless to say.

I haven't seen Simon since he turned up out of the blue on that Wednesday in March. I chose not to mention it to Vivien. If she'd known about it, it'd have been her he would have come round to see. She would have kept me away from the sordid misery of that evening. No, it was a deliberate choice to approach me in order to see Geoff.

He did come to the game. I had a couple of stewards check that the seat had been used. He left at half time, though, possibly once he realised that I'd still managed to keep him away from the family. From actually having the chance to see Geoff up close. I have a feeling that it might not be the last I'll see of him. I've already got to a point where I keep thinking I see him on every street corner. Following me. Watching.

Giving him the ticket felt a little like paying off a blackmailer. A way of paying him off permanently would be to prove I was Geoff's father. Failing that, the only alternatives would be to get a restraining order, and then I'd have to prove he was being a menace, or to find some hold over him that balanced the situation, that could promise to keep him away.

The nineties had been almost entirely forgettable for West Ham United. I'd had a daydream when Alan Devonshire left the club in October 1998 that Geoff Hurst might eschew a return to the world of double glazing in favour of offering himself up for a management job at Upton Park. He didn't, but they did find a name from the past to take over the running of the club. That was Tony Cottee, the prolific striker from the mid-eighties, who was winding down after a brilliant career at Villa Park, where he had finished as the top division's top striker for three successive seasons in the eighties. His career stats, scoring 189 goals in 458 appearances, had made him the third-highest Aston Villa goalscorer of all time. He was still only 33 when he came to West Ham as manager, and like Bonds and Devonshire before him, great things were hoped of him for the future.

This time something clicked. It might have been the master stroke of dragging two of his ex-colleagues, the 34 year old Alan Dickens and Keith McPherson, out of semi-retirement to play the season of their lives. With Cottee putting on his boots, too, it had the look of a re-incarnated Hammers side from the eighties. Dickens had to lose nearly a stone to get fit, though McPherson, who had been playing for Reading, was probably fitter than both of them, and still playing regularly. Cottee put together an effective if not particularly sprightly team in just three weeks, determined to take them up to the new First Division.

West Ham First XI, 1998-99: Neil Sullivan, Keith McPherson, Julian Dicks, Rio Ferdinand, Steve Potts, Alan Dickens, Joe Cole, Emmanuel Omoyinmi, Frank Lampard, Tony Cottee, Iain Dowie. Substitute: Scott Mean.

The combination of young and old was exactly right for the division West Ham were trying to get out of. With its long ballers and tactic spoilers, its Wrexhams, Wigans and Colchesters, it soon became obvious to Cottee just why West Ham had languished in that league under Alan Devonshire. Teams with class would have to muck in and get their hands dirty, and the combination of old pros who had learned all the tricks in the book and the young hopefuls who didn't know any different, soon had the Hammers rushing up the table to the top by January 1999.

The Hammers' Youth Academy was the other ace up Cottee's sleeve, providing him with Rio Ferdinand at the centre of defence and the brilliant midfield skills of Emmanuel Omoyinmi and the young Joe Cole, not forgetting the industry of Frank Lampard Jnr. They walked away with the Second Division title that season, winning it by an astonishing fourteen clear points. Although they were still only in the First Division after promotion, the volume of wins and goals scored, even at that level, had Upton Park filled to capacity for every game. The improved gates meant that loans could easily be secured on the amount necessary to complete the building of the West Stand, and conversion of the ground to an all seater stadium for the first time in its history.

Cottee, McPherson and Dickens would now retire from playing, but would collectively become the core coaching staff, their experience on the pitch guaranteeing a clear perspective on what it might take to return this famous old club to the new Primary League. It was a League in which they were yet to compete, but for which they looked as ready as they had ever been in the last ten years.

Just when it had almost gone out of my mind, he's back. I hear the knock at the door and I look at my phone. March 30th 2001. It's one year to the day since he was last here. That's psychopathic. I think about pretending I'm not in, but it's no use. I know he saw me when I pulled the curtain back.

What does the fucker want?

I look towards the utility room and see the boxes of stuff we've got lined up for Geoff's twenty-first on Sunday.

That's what he wants. He's going to do this every year until … Until what?

'What do you want?'

'Let me in. Just for a few minutes. You don't want the neighbours seeing a row on the doorstep do you?' He's already taken the initiative and walked boldly into the house like he owns the place.

'What do you want?'

'A meeting. Can we meet somewhere, all of us?'

He takes a long puff on his cigarette, and I change my mind.

'Come and sit down,' I say, surprised at the calm sound of my voice. 'Can I get you a tea?'

'No thanks. I just want, you know, to sort something out. A chance for us all to meet.'

He seems more nervous than he was last time. Unpredictable.

'I thought we agreed that when you had gone to the match, that would be it.'

'I didn't agree anything. But thank you for the ticket. It was good to see the game. He's not a bad player.'

'Playing for Chelsea now,' I say. 'He's got his own flat, though. He doesn't live here.'

'I know. That's why you'll have to arrange something.'

'I'll need your mobile number and your address.'

'There's my mobile.' He pushes a torn piece of paper at me with his number on it. I dial it straight away. He looks at me with a confused, angry expression. The phone rings in his pocket.

'You don't trust me.'

'Look at it from my point of view. As far as I'm concerned, you're this mad bloke who comes to the house once a year in the hope that he can talk to someone who might or might not be his son. It's not a very normal way to behave. Why can't you contact Vivien? She was the one you fucked, after all. Or are you trying to fuck me now?'

'Vivien was very rude to me last time we talked. You are a better route to Geoff. It can be done without anyone getting upset. Geoff doesn't need to know who I am, providing you make the whole thing seem normal. A meeting by chance with an old friend.'

'Viv would kill you if she knew you were here. I didn't tell her about your last visit.'

'That's why you'll organise a meeting with just the three of us. I can be one of your friends.'

'And how do I know you won't be back next year?'

'You've got my number. You could call the police. If you'd organised this properly last year I wouldn't be here now. I just want to talk to him. Ring me when you've sorted something out in the next fortnight. You can call me Tony when we talk. Less risk.'

I see him to the door and watch him leave. He walks to the road. If he has a car, he's left it out of sight. Maybe I should tell Viv this time. But then, maybe not. She'll want to know why I didn't tell her before. And I don't know the answer to that question.

Wimbledon are down.

The first few years of the 'noughties' as they have been christened by the press that loves to divide our lives up into decades – and it's back to West Ham's fortunes being inversely proportional to mine. The Dons finally dropped out of the Primary League in May 2000, and I left the club two weeks later. Of the nine main newspapers, six of them said I was sacked, even though I put in my resignation to the board the day after the last game against Villa. Apart from a two minute piece I do for GB on Sky to deny it, I don't bother. 'Sacked' makes a better story than 'Resigned', whatever the truth is, so there seems little point arguing. For all I know, the Board put out the story.

I get the departure package I'm after, and Gary has promised me some work on Sky to keep the wolverhamptons away from the door. The overwhelming feeling I have is of relief. I am only 46, and football has been good to me. There were times during the fight against relegation in the last few games, particularly after the unexpected 1-0 home win over Chelsea, when I was thinking – even if we stay up, I'll still have to leave! – but in the end the decision was made for me, and I'm not too disappointed. Tomorrow's Wimbledon will be someone else's legacy.

Tony Cottee is on a run and a roll and his 1999-2000 Hammers leap up into the Primary League at the very first opportunity, though they have to settle for second behind Kevin Keegan's runaway leaders Fulham. There's not much of him, TC, but he has been all the things as a manager for the side that Bonds and Devonshire couldn't be. Then again, he has been given access to players like Cole, Lampard and Ferdinand, all of whom are staying on at the club for another season in the light of both their contracts and West Ham's promotion to the top division. Cottee has another midfield star for the future in South Shields born Michael Carrick, who has come to the fore in 2000, again through the Youth Academy.

GB has put me in touch with a man from Sectogene, a company dealing with the kind of science I currently have a profound interest in. After that lunatic left on his last visit, I had some serious thinking to do. Gary's the only one I've told about Simon's visits. GB wasn't prepared to give me advice, but he's found what I asked him to. Sectogene offer a choice of services. There is a Private Home Testing kit, which shows DNA matches from different samples, and there is a legal challenge-proof service performed in the company's laboratories that is certified for court. It makes sense to go for the second choice, even though it's a hell of a lot more expensive.

Geoff's twenty-first wasn't the celebration I wanted it to be. I found myself looking outside every so often to see if he would show. The other aspect of the evening that spoiled it for me was deciding what I should take of his for DNA. Now I've got myself emotionally embroiled in all of this, it feels like I'm no better than Simon. I have suddenly been given the opportunity of discovering whether my son is really my son. I'm not even sure any more if I am doing this to get Simon off my back, or to finally find out for good.

The problems don't end with the taking of the test. What will I do if Simon is the father? I'll have to arrange that meeting and hope he's as good as his word. Will I be clever enough to hide the knowledge from him, once I have it? Even at the age of twenty-one, Geoff has no idea about the paternity issues surrounding his birth. Viv and I took a decision that that was how it would be. Forever. I've tried imagining how I might have taken that kind of news when I was twenty-one, if my father had told me. No matter how empathetic I may fancy myself

186

to be, I am not him. I can only know once I've told him, and then it may be too late.

Luckily Geoff stays over after the party. I take the comb from his toiletries bag when he's asleep and put it in some clingfilm with the cigarette butt Simon left in the driveway after his visit. As for me, I cut a lock of my hair, so the items are clearly separate. The company is based in Basingstoke, but I have to drop the items off at a private clinic on their books in Raynes Park. The results will be back in 3-5 days. Why do I feel like a criminal? I'm not the psychopath making unannounced home visits ...

Two days after I've sent the samples off, I get a phone call on the mobile that sounds official and sombre.

'Is that Roy Nolan?'

'Yes.'

'This is West Middlesex Hospital. We were given your name by a Gary Benchman.'

'Bentley.'

'Yes. It's about Charlie Barth. He's a friend of yours?'

I feel sickeningly relieved that the call isn't the announcement of prematurely processed lab results, but feel a cramp in my stomach about Charlie.

I sit by his bed throughout the night. Charlie has had a massive heart attack and is on a life support machine. He is only alive because of the youth of his body, a testimony to his days in football. Even so, they have no idea whether or not he will recover, and even if he does, things might not be working. Brain, liver, heart, kidney. Things the body can't do without.

I'm picking up the bill for the room. I can't have him in a public ward just in case the press get hold of the story. He's had a few bad pieces written about him over the years.

I go home to change and Vivien is there.

'Will he die?'

'I don't know, love. No-one seems to know. Sometimes it's good not to know.'

'Are you going back?'

'His parents are coming over from South Africa tomorrow. I'm going to stay with him until then.' She hugs me and I feel like a fraud. This woman who called me a fake once before. I am still a fake.

Back at the hospital I've put the phone on silent. The other news could come today. Funny that I'll probably be getting it sitting next to

Charlie, morphine and tubed up on a machine. A lot of life changing due in the next day or two.

I watch him lying there. I'd done that a couple of times when he'd stayed over at the flat. He always fell asleep instantly, while I'd spend the night turning and turning. Even when things were going okay I'd find little ideas and wrongdoings creeping round my head like mosquitoes.

The phone finally starts vibrating. It's an 'Unknown' number.

'Excuse me, Charlie,' I say to the empty room.

I take the call in the corridor.

'Mr Nolan? Can I have your full address, date of birth and Sectogene password?'

I give them the information. My throat has gone birdcage dry.

'This is the Sectogene Laboratories in Basingstoke. We have the results of your DNA tests. Would you like them now on the phone, or would you like them sent by e-mail?'

I wonder momentarily at the logic of their practice.

'Now, on the phone, please.'

'Very well. We have the labelled items A, B and C and I can confirm that there is no match.'

'I'm sorry? No match? Nothing matches across all three samples?'

'Yes,' she says frostily. 'That's what 'no match' means.'

'Thank you. Bye.'

I wander back into Charlie's room, and I am crying. I have no idea why. The point is, Simon is not Roger's father. That's for certain. I can tell him that. I will tell him that. He will not be coming back again.

But I'm not the father either. The father is an American. Someone who doesn't even know he has a son back in England, playing football for Chelsea. A brilliant footballer who may go to the very top of his profession.

I was never interested in finding out until that sad fucker came round. Never wanted to. Never needed to. And now I know, will it change me? Will it change us? I have a terrible secret that I may have to take with me to the grave.

I look at Charlie lying there, in a bliss of unconsciousness, detached from the world.

He looks happy.

One of the reasons Chloe and I stopped seeing each other was because she met this top designer Aver-something-o, his name was. Averreccio?

Something like that. She wanted us to still meet up when she came to London, but I stopped it. I didn't want to, but it wasn't fair on her, or him or me. In the end, I had to let her go. There's only one of me and one of her, and monogamy makes more sense in the end. You get tired of dodging bullets and making up stories in your head that you end up forgetting. It didn't stop me thinking of her every day. I still do. But thinking is less tiring than acting out.

Her thing with Averreccio didn't lead to anything in the end, but I read in the *Telegraph* last week that she is marrying Carlos Moravia, the managing director of the Moravio fashion house. That's about right for her. She won't be short of anything, though she could probably buy him a few houses, too.

The timing was never quite right for us, but we met, and we had a good time. I won't forget her.

By the end of 2000-01, Tony Cottee has secured a remarkable eighth position in the Primary League with the Hammers, in just his third season in charge. Whether he can hang on to the big four as they now are, remains to be seen. There have been silly money offers for all four players, though they are all figures that have been paid for foreign internationals before this season. Ferdinand and Lampard are already training with the full England squad, and it won't be long before they are joined by Cole. West Ham can fund their East Stand by just selling one of them. No-one could blame the club after three of the most successful years in its history.

		P	W	D	L	F	A	Pts
1	Man United	38	24	8	6	72	31	80
2	Arsenal	38	23	6	9	65	32	75
3	Liverpool	38	21	6	11	72	40	69
4	Ipswich	38	18	9	11	52	33	63
5	Sunderland	38	17	11	10	49	32	62
6	Sheff Utd	38	17	10	11	63	45	61
7	Southampton	38	18	7	13	60	47	61
8	West Ham	38	16	13	9	62	50	61

GB had lent me the keys to his flat in Worthing. It wasn't the most prestigious getaway corner of the globe, but as he had said when we'd first discussed it, that was part of its charm. I chucked the pushbike in the back of the 4x4 and headed down the M23 towards the South Downs.

West Sussex was a county I knew very little about. It had often been referred to as the Garden of England, along with several other counties including Surrey and Kent, but once I'd got off the motorway, it started to look a little bit more deserving of its shared second name. Once in Worthing, I drove into town and parked just along from the pier. The summer heat hit me with a thump as I got out of the air-conditioned car. It was nearly half seven, and the streets were deserted of shoppers and tourists, but there was still that pleasant atmosphere of holiday in the smell of the sea air.

The beach was pebble and shingle, so I abandoned the thoughts I'd had of going for a shoeless stroll, and headed over to the front of the pier. Marine Parade. Seaside towns. Quintessentially English. A part of our strange culture that America had yet to breach. I stopped at the Worthing Pavilion, or the Pavilion Theatre, as the sign in the lobby area read.

It was the last face I expected to see in that remote part of England, far from my world of football, crowds and floodlights. 'An Evening With Geoff Hurst – You Didn't Mean To Do That, Did You?' Recollections from the career of one of England's unsung football heroes and the top TV football pundit star of *Saint and Hurstie*.

My plan had been for a pint and some fish and chips, but this seemed worth a look. The woman in the box office was texting someone on her mobile and jumped when I tapped on the glass.

'It's the next door for the pier,' she said. 'Though it closes at eight tonight.'

'What about Hurstie?'

'What do you mean?'

'The show. Has it already started?'

'Go on,' she said. 'I had a couple of returns earlier.' She pushed the tickets at me and smiled. I wondered if she even knew who Hurstie was. I took the tickets, though why she'd given me two wasn't clear, and went past her through the curtain to the back of the stalls.

The theatre was half full, but all heads were pointed at the stage, captivated by what was being said. Hurstie was wearing his customary blue blazer and grey slacks with his red striped 1966 World Cup Winners tie.

The tie was pinned to his shirt by a gold tiepin, just below his chest. There was something faintly ridiculous about him, yet lovable all the same. One of the characteristics of his success as alter ego Hurstie had been his ability to chuckle at himself after he's said something, as if he couldn't believe he was doing what he was doing. As if he had come from another world where he didn't have to send himself up like this, where he had achieved notoriety from a position of unique achievement. From a world where the linesman's flag had pointed at the centre circle and not the goal-line.

I took a seat about three rows back from the last full row, detached but enthralled by the story I had walked in on. It was Hurst's recollection of how he had driven into the ITV studios a couple of weeks before the new football season in 1992-93, only to discover that the room he and Saint had used for nearly seven years to prepare ideas for their programme had been turned into a men's room.

'I found myself pissing just where I'd always been pissing myself.'

He had a dry, quietly spoken delivery, which made a lot of what he said even funnier, not least because of the self-deprecating sniggers and shaking of the head.

Incredible, I was thinking. In my dream as a twelve year old, this man had hit a hat-trick for England in the World Cup Final. He had done something no-one had ever done before or since. A stunning moment in world football, something even Pele had not achieved. But because of the wave of a linesman's flag and a referee's decision, this man is spending his time talking to a few hundred people in a small hall by the side of Worthing Pier.

My own career might look as impressive as Hurst's in the history books, but when I look at him I am a nervous kid again, out in the backyard, juggling a ball in the air towards the 100 pay-off, defying my dad by looking east instead of up the Seven Sisters Road, by taking the Upton Park oath and by supporting, as they are today, Tony Cottee's claret and blue army.

Hurst ends the show by offering the audience questions from the floor. A man with a microphone on the end of a pole has obviously been hired to point it at the person asking the question, but Hurst waves him away when it becomes clear that there isn't going to be a difficulty with the acoustics.

'Can you hear us at the back?' Hurst shouts towards me. I raise my hand to indicate clear reception. How strange that I should end up here when I drove down to get away from football.

The questions come thick and fast, and Hurst's replies are as poignant as they are amusing. He has clearly realised that television has made him something of a national treasure in spite of missing out in the World Cup Final, 40 years ago. Eventually a question is asked by an old lady in the front row, who Hurst almost breaks his back bending down to hear.

'What's your best memory, Geoff, from football, before you became successful in television?'

Hurst reflects for a few seconds before replying.

'It isn't the obvious one. Appearing in a World Cup Final is something every footballer wants to do, whoever they are, however good they are. But when you get to wherever you get to in football, if the fame takes you into the public eye, then you have a special kind of responsibility. Some years after the World Cup Final, towards the end of my career at West Ham, I went to see the kids, the under-18s, playing in an FA Youth Cup Quarter Final at Upton Park.

'I wasn't in the team. I hadn't been playing for a while, but I went. I wanted to see maybe some stars of the future. West Ham were playing Crystal Palace, I think it was, and they lost 2-0. Afterwards, when we were having some food in the directors' lounge, they let the kids in. They were all excited, as you'd imagine, mixing with some famous footballers. Sir Trevor Brooking was there, for a start. And I'm sat in the corner, and this kid on the Palace side, their best player on the night by a mile he was, said to me: 'It was because of you that I took up football seriously.' I was gobsmacked. That's all he said.

'I thought about it later, driving back home. That's it, I thought. This game's as much about the people who watch it as the achievements of those who they watch. And that little kid met his hero that night and said what he said. That's good enough for me, I thought. That's good enough for me.'

I'm sitting in the car now, eating a rather large portion of fish and chips. To think that I might have missed that moment if I hadn't come down here for the evening. To think that for the whole length of my career, that was the only time I ever played football on the pitch at Upton Park. To think that on that day I also met my hero, Geoff Hurst.

No-one listens to you when you're a kid. That's what I used to think. But I was wrong. Hurstie listened, and he noticed me, even when I thought he hadn't.

From kicking a ball in the backyard to managing a team for ten years in the top league in the world, it's been quite a life. Lucky just to have been in the right place at the right time, and to have had the chance to take advantage of it all.

Football is my life – and Geoff Hurst gave it to me.